Cooking

Trailside Cooking

Russ Mohney

STACKPOLE BOOKS

TRAILSIDE COOKING

Published by
STACKPOLE BOOKS
Cameron and Kelker Streets
P.O. Box 1831
Harrisburg, PA. 17105

Printed in the U.S.A.

Library of Congress Cataloging in Publication Data

Mohney, Russ.
  Trailside cooking.

  1. Outdoor cookery. I. Title.
TX823.M64   641.5'78   76-14417
ISBN 0-8117-2264-3

Contents

Preface

There are several factors involved in every outdoor adventure that ultimately determine the overall success of the experience. A few of these are completely beyond control of the outdoorsman, who must rely on some benevolent good fortune to provide sunshine, cooling breezes, fair fishing, and perfect scenery. Many more of these ingredients vital to happiness in the field are fortunately quite within our control. With proper planning and execution we can assure ourselves of comfortable sleeping accommodations, protection from adverse elements, good comradeship, and memorable eating along the way.

Of all these controllable factors, probably none

rates higher than trailside cookery to the final success of the outing. Certainly a warm sleeping bag is a comfort on a chilly night, and a snug shelter against a two-day rainstorm helps make it all bearable—but an attractive and nourishing hot meal makes even the worst of outings a lot less traumatic. Long after the pictures have been pasted in the scrapbook, you'll still remember Charlie's chicken soup on that blustery afternoon. Sure, it might have been diluted by the rain dripping off your nose, but it will be recalled as the high point of that special day!

Since the very dawn of mankind, food (and the search for it) has been one of the driving forces shaping civilization. By modern definition, a backward society is one without enough to eat. The development of a massive agricultural establishment in our age notwithstanding, much of modern life still centers on the individual dinner table. It is true, perhaps, that today's urban population is largely unfamiliar with a plow or hoe—and that a gigantic industry has been built around supermarket packaging and "convenience" foods. Still, we dedicate much of our working life to securing, preparing, and eating our food. Although most of us don't give it due thought, a lot of marriages, divorces, contracts, and other social/business achievements are consummated around the supper table. Food has become much more than a simple refueling process;

it is a vital element in the enjoyment of life. No-
where is that more true than along the trail.

Not so many years ago, food in the outdoor camp
was called "grub," a name that fairly well described
the flour-and-bean nightmares that were thrown
together in enormous iron skillets, cooked to the
consistency of asphalt shingles, and slapped onto
a tin plate to be choked down by a motley assortment of surveyors, trappers, and other antisocial
types. About the only compliment ever heard was,
"It'll stick to your ribs!" It would also stick to your
spoon, your mess kit, your galoshes, and anything
else you happened to spill it on. Manfully gulped
down with only a few caustic comments about the
cook's ancestry, this "grub" would lay like a sodden
lump in the stomach for several hours, allegedly
providing sufficient energy to accomplish the no-
toriously hard work that characterized that era. The
workingman's constitution (and digestive juices)
were a lot stronger then, and "grub" was about the
most accurate word around to describe it.

The cooking utensils of that fortunately bygone
day were just about as rustic as the menu—and just
about as unsuited to the present-day hiker. The
kitchen was assembled around a giant iron skillet,
often three feet in diameter and weighing upwards
of sixty pounds. A couple of anonymous long-
handled scrapers, a clanging assortment of cast-
iron pots, and a sheet metal reflector oven completed

the set. It wasn't very sophisticated, but neither was the mule required to carry it all!

The modern backpacker has a whole new arsenal of foods and utensils at his fingertips, adding variety, taste, nutrition, and ease to the trailside fare. Yesterday's meals were a monotonous mass of shapeless and tasteless conglomerates. The only way to tell breakfast from dinner was with your watch! The current hiker, however, has a choice that ranges from beans-and-bacon to turkey tetrazzini. Camp cooking has progressed from the barbaric to the artistic, and words like "grub" and "Belly-robber" have all but passed from usage.

It is now possible for otherwise civilized people to head into the woods with just a few pounds of food and gear, live comfortably and eat well for two weeks, and return without scurvy, protein deficiency, or bellies distended by carbohydrate malnutrition. Eating along the trail need no longer be a simple matter of survival—it can become the vital factor of enjoyment it rightfully deserves to be. By knowing the elementary nutritional requirements, the food combinations available, and the best techniques of preparation, even the most hopeless of kitchen dolts can create beautiful and delicious meals on the trail. His simple skills over the camp stove can enrich the experience for everyone involved, adding a new dimension to the joy of hiking and camping.

Above all else, the camp meal is inseparably woven into the fabric of the moment. The sights, sounds, and smells of the wilderness are subtle spices simmered into every meal, giving each bite a savor that cannot be found in the finest of inns or dining halls. When the stew is gently blended of equal parts meat, vegetable, birdsong, sunshine, and the fragrance of pines, it is a feast unduplicated by the masters of cuisine. Garnished with friendship and freedom, it is a steaming gift from the gods, feeding the spirit every bit as effectively as it feeds the body.

1

The Ritual of Eating

Throughout history, the various societies of mankind have placed great ritualistic emphasis on the act of eating. The development of agriculture has always had a bearing on the progress of nations, since the ability to feed a population has separated the rich from the poor, the weak from the strong. On a global basis, the efficient production of food has determined which countries would rule their part of the world.

It isn't strange, then, that ancient rulers made the act of eating a special part of their folklore, celebrations, and religion. When an heir to a royal family was born, a day of feasting and revelry was decreed, and the people allowed extra rations as a gesture of fulfillment. The Roman civilization made feasting and revelry an important social and political function, to such an extent that the middle class was taxed beyond its ability to pay in order to support the extravagance of the rich and powerful.

In early America the survival of the first settlers was marked by an enormous feast to which the Indians were invited. Although it had religious overtones, the first Thanksgiving was almost pagan in nature, as sorely-needed food stores were broken out and consumed in the face of impending winter. The ingrained social custom of feasting seemed more important than the prospect of starvation in the bleak months ahead.

A noted anthropologist has theorized that our primitive ancestors felt something akin to pleasure only through eating or sex. Not yet an agricultural beast, early man was a hunter and a gatherer, depending on benign Nature and dumb luck to keep his belly full. Through countless centuries of progress and evolution, man has expanded his list of pleasurable activities many times, but eating still stands at the top of the list. (A close second, perhaps?)

As recently as the turn of the century, our society still placed great emphasis on the quality and quantity of our food. Boardinghouses were judged by their meals rather than the softness of the beds or the distance to the privy, and transient cowpunchers rated a given ranch more on the skill of the cook than pay scales or working conditions. Instant

entertainment and mass advertising were still in the future, so the daily dinner remained the focal point of human activity and enjoyment.

Somewhere in the preposterous emergence of agri-business and enormous marketing centers, the joy of eating got lost—and we are all the poorer for it. In the pressure of a speed-oriented society, eating has become a perfunctory gesture, accomplished at the greatest possible speed and with the least possible taste. Giant chains of hamburger stands and chicken stores pride themselves on the ability to coax you in, put their greasy plastic food in your stomach, and get you back on the street in twenty-four seconds flat. Whether the food provides enjoyment or nourishment is immaterial, so long as the cash register keeps dinging!

The past two decades have seen a return of the people to the land, a return to ways more primitive than we're accustomed to. The parks, forests, and wildernesses are groaning under the press of millions of people who seek relaxation and recreation far from the sounds of society. Scientists and sociologists point out dozens of reasons for this renaissance of the outdoor life, but they might be missing the boat. There's a vast difference between a stew simmered slowly and carefully beside a tumbling creek and 12-second microwave chicken (sodium ascorbate added to retard spoilage)—and the difference goes far beyond science and sociology. It is a distinction found on the taste buds of the soul!

The overall enjoyment of any outdoor adventure—from an afternoon walk in a nearby woodlot to a month spent rambling through a skyline wilderness—depends on a great many factors. Our food, whether it be a knapsack lunch or a two-hour dinner, is one of the most vital of these. Even the dreary discomfort of a dismal day can be brightened by a busy, bubbling pot of soup under a balsam shelter. Long after the memories of the rain and wind have softened, a warm recollection of the heady aroma and bright flavor will remain. Under the best of conditions a camp dinner is an indelible picture that will remain in our memory as long as we live. The delicate shades of twilight remain pure and vivid against the years as we return to that special supper of golden trout, crisp potatoes, and steaming greens. If anything, the meal gets better with every recollection.

Although the camp dinner is an inseparable element of our enjoyment, it serves another function no less important. It is through our food that we keep our bodies fueled, efficient, and comfortable. Among the special factors that lead to joy and happiness in the field are our ability to be comfortably mobile, and the extent to which we can produce the unusual amounts of energy needed to perform unaccustomed work. By understanding the physical needs of our bodies during this period of accelerated activity and properly ministering to these needs, we enhance the whole experience.

Finally, our food along the trail becomes part of an experience that can only be described as "spiritual," fulfilling an inner need that is often absent in the social environment. The private little moments spent stirring our food give us time for reflection. After dinner each utensil is washed, dried, and returned to its special place in our pack with a degree of care unthought of at home: another moment for thought. Even the minutes and hours after the meal are devoted to afterthoughts of the food and to calm digestion. Far from jangling telephones, haranguing television, or the insidious sounds and smells of the parking lot, we are quiet and secure within the cloistered confines of our chosen camp. We have narrowed the limits of our personal world, lessened the pressures we must bear, and allowed ourselves the opportunity to thoroughly enjoy a simple meal.

One of the first changes that occurs when we forsake the comfort of a concrete cliff-dwelling for the trail is an acute awareness of the body we have for so long taken for granted. This sensitivity is initially exhibited in the twinges and aches of misused muscles returning to productive life. After a short period of readjustment, we begin to feel our movements differently, as the channels of communication between unused muscles and less-used portions of our brain awaken. After the first shocks of returning to a largely physical existence, we begin feeling a new strength and vitality that are at once exhilarating and confusing. With the growing awareness of our physical body there is a growing appetite as we shrug off the imbalances caused by too little exercise, stale air, diesel fumes, and a diet dictated by advertising and convenience instead of common sense. The food we will eat during this marvelous period will keep our bodies working efficiently, our spirits soaring above the clouds, and ourselves more alert to the beauty and joy around us. At these times it isn't unusual to see a normally officebound middle-ager pick up an eighty-pound rock *just for the fun of feeling his muscles work!* When a few days have passed and our bodies are once again functioning as they were designed to function, we may feel a bit giddy and understandably proud of the way we react to physical demands. That's part of the fun. Our bodies should work perfectly for a lot longer than most of us realize—don't be surprised when they do!

Many hikers in this youth-oriented world are amazed that a person of forty or fifty can cover miles of trail with relative ease. They are astounded that a person of sixty can walk several miles without a massive coronary, and are absolutely astonished that a gentleman of seventy would have the audacity to leave his front porch, much less shoulder a respectable pack and venture into the wilderness. Nonetheless, thousands of hikers and backpackers in this country reach the golden years without the least intention of spending them in a rocking chair.

I once was asked to guide a charming old gentleman and his party into the high Cascades for a late-summer outing. A retired officer of the U.S. Fish and Wildlife Service, this man had spent the best part of fifty summers studying the life in those mountains. Although he was nearly eighty at the time, the thought never crossed his mind that he should give up his favorite pastime: walking the trails of the high country.

The only concession he made to his age was allowing his two sons-in-law, both of whom were M.D.'s, to join the group. The trip was to be strictly a backpack expedition; he hated motor vehicles and wasn't too thrilled with horses. The nearest thing I had to pack mules were two young men on the brink of their twentieth summer. They had had plenty of experience with the mountains, but never in the company of a doddering old-timer like our guest. I'm quite certain they thought the whole trip would be an ordeal, accomplished at a snail's pace. Without going into detail, let me assure you that the rest of our party practically had to run to keep up with the old fellow. By the time we returned to timberline, my two young companions had learned a great deal—not the least of which was respect.

I must admit that this gentleman was not an average case. He was capable of more hiking than many people half his age, having long ago learned to treat his body correctly, eat properly, and worry only about those things that deserve it. It's a combination that is pretty hard to beat.

The simple fact is that the foods we eat are uniquely responsible for our health, strength, and ability to enjoy the outdoors for many years. The foods we eat along the trail are necessary for immediate energy, but we must maintain a reasonable diet throughout the year if we want to extend our trail years beyond middle age. A healthy, balanced diet for a few weeks in the summer just isn't enough. The nutritional guidelines in the next chapter are important, of course, for the trail, but they are just as important the rest of the time.

Before we go any further, let me hasten to point out that I am neither a food faddist nor a qualified nutritionist. You won't find much wheat germ, protein pills, or yogurt in this book, since they aren't particularly suited (or necessary) for trailside cookery. The nutritional elements presented are compiled from accepted sources and have been checked by a fully-qualified graduate nutritionist. All the foods listed here are readily available at the corner supermarket or the outfitter's shop—you won't have to visit the neighborhood health food store for the ingredients. If, on the other hand, you regularly include specialized health foods in your diet at home, use them on the trail. Other than their being a bit overpriced and not particularly necessary for the average trail menu, I don't have anything against them.

With the great array of products on the market suitable for trail cookery, the backpack menu need not be either monotonous or restricted. You can eat the foods you like, achieve a fine nutritional balance, and have fun doing it. That's really what it's all about.

One final aspect of trailside cookery must be examined carefully, and we will consider it in each of the food types or combinations included. That is, of course, the cost and weight ratios of various foods in relation to the nutritional and flavor benefits derived from them. Many of the foods developed for backpackers—particularly the freeze-dried meats—are prohibitively expensive. Some of the less expensive supermarket foods are just too heavy to carry, and at least a few foods are unsuitable because they tend to spoil rather quickly in a warm pack. None of these factors should be allowed to interfere with the enjoyment of the outing. It is quite possible, as we shall see, to strike a good compromise between cost and weight without giving up pleasure or nutrition along the way.

The young couple on a budget cannot choose their diet as if money were no concern, and they will likely have to carry a little heavier pack, but they can still whip up a series of appealing and nourishing meals on the trail. For the majority of us, the trail menu will be a combination of freeze-dried and traditional foods, providing excellent nutrients with a reasonable balance between cost and weight. With the guides presented in this book, you should be able to select foods that will suit your own taste without putting an undue weight on your back or drain on your pocketbook.

The backpacker has a wide choice in the utensils he will use in his trailside kitchen. Some of the ultralight gear is terribly expensive, but some of the low cost equipment is either much too heavy or of poor quality. In the appropriate chapter we will discuss the options available (including some do-it-yourself items that can be made for a few pennies) to keep one's trip within budgetary limitations. The choice of cooking gear, incidentally, has a great deal to do with the various recipes and combinations you will use in the field. A lot of hikers, for example, are beginning to depend heavily on the ancient Chinese wok for the majority of their meals. This superb utensil adapts particularly well to the one-burner backpack stove, produces some really outstanding meals with ease, and incorporates an economy of ingredients that has become legendary in rural China.

Innovative designs in equipment and packaging have appeared that make life a lot easier for the wilderness chef, and there has been a lot of inventive experimentation with simple foods from other societies—all of which has expanded our own opportunities for fun and good taste as we hike.

It is now possible to carry enough food into the wilderness to last for several weeks while providing all the variety and flavor one could ask. There will still be those who endure the drab monotony of the same foods over and over, but many hikers are discovering the wealth of new tastes that may be found on every supermarket shelf. Those who are willing to experiment a little, to depart from a self-imposed routine, will find that their mealtime has indeed become a vital factor in the enjoyment of the outdoors.

2

Calories
and Cauliflowers

The science of nutrition has become very exact and detailed, yet even the most casual observer must discover the wide differences of opinion among the experts as to what comprises a proper diet. About once a week a new book appears on the market purporting to lead the reader to the verdant fields of good health, heightened awareness, and a pimple-free complexion. Some of these wonder diets promise you'll lose fifty pounds in a couple of weeks, or shift fifty pounds from one place to another. Each of these diets enjoys a flash of popularity, then fades into well-deserved obscurity. In the end, the dieter either gets on a stable, reasonable schedule of reduced intake or resigns himself to packing around that excess weight until something else comes along. A few people are concerned with gaining some poundage, but most are looking to shed a little. Someone once observed that there can't be too much wrong with the economy of a country whose biggest problems are losing weight and finding a place to park! That seems to be a situation shared by those of us who look for our recreation out of doors.

Actually, most hikers and backpackers are not terribly concerned with a weight-loss diet, as least while they are on an outdoor trip. The combination of increased energy output and essentially balanced foods makes weight gain less a problem

along the trail. Our chief concern will be developing a diet that will maintain a high energy level despite the increased physical activity.

The National Academy of Science has devised a list of recommended daily dietary allowances (the RDA) that pretty effectively outlines how much of which basic nutrients a person needs to keep well and fit. The RDA specifies certain levels of foods for different ages and body types under normal conditions. Unfortunately, hiking and backpacking are far from normal activities, so certain adjustments must be made on the basis of the degree of physical exertion, weather conditions, elevation, and other variable factors. Still, the recommended daily allowances give us a place to begin thinking about our refueling needs on the trail. The accompanying chart is the 1973 revised version of the RDA.

As you can see, there is quite a wide difference between the requirements for certain groups of people, and none of the figures can be considered exact. The RDA is periodically revised by the National Academy of Science on the basis of new data and experiments in human nutrition. From a purely practical standpoint, it is quite impossible to say how many calories a day will be enough, or how many grams of protein are necesary to rebuild body cells. It really isn't critical to regulate the diet quite that closely, anyway. If we get enough to eat without overloading our digestive system, and the foods we choose are effectively balanced, there will be no great difficulty in achieving the required energy levels.

The question of vitamins and minerals along the trail is of little interest to the average backpacker, since his stay in the wilderness is usually of fairly short duration. Normal reserves and vitamins taken through normal foods should be plenty. If there is any cause for concern, the hiker can supplement his diet with one of the common multiple-vitamin capsules from the corner druggist.

Although arguments will probably swirl around the difference between natural and synthetic vitamins, the One-A-Day-Tablet® vitamin supplements are really quite efficient for the backpacker. They insure him of ample essential vitamins, yet don't require him to carry foods that are difficult to transport or prepare. Many women will find the iron-fortified capsules a good choice for the correspondingly higher iron requirements outlined by the RDA.

With the question of vitamins and minerals settled by the use of supplemental capsules, we can concentrate on the three essential building blocks of energy for the hiker: protein, carbohydrates, and fats. It is important to note that the balance of protein, carbohydrates, and fats becomes more critical as the trip gets longer. For a weekend jaunt or a few days in the wilderness the nutritional considerations are minimal. If all you care to carry are tea and chocolate bars, that should be no trouble over the short

RECOMMENDED DAILY DIETARY ALLOWANCES[1], REVISED 1973

Designed for the maintenance of good nutrition of practically all healthy people in the U.S.A.

	(years) From Up to	Weight (kg)	Weight (lbs)	Height (cm)	Height (in)	Energy (kcal)[2]	Protein (g)	Fat-Soluble Vitamins Vitamin A Activity (RE)[3]	Vitamin A Activity (IU)	Vitamin D (IU)	Vitamin E Activity[5] (IU)
INFANTS	0.0-0.5	6	14	60	24	kg x 117	kg x 2.2	420[4]	1400	400	4
	0.5-1.0	9	20	71	28	kg x 108	kg x 2.0	400	2000	400	5
CHILDREN	1-3	13	28	86	34	1300	23	400	2000	400	7
	4-6	20	44	110	44	1800	30	500	2500	400	9
	7-10	30	66	135	54	2400	36	700	3300	400	10

	(kg)	(lb)	(cm)	(in)	kcal	(g)				
MALES										
11-14	44	97	158	63	2800	44	1000	5000	400	12
15-18	61	134	172	69	3000	54	1000	5000	400	15
19-22	67	147	172	69	3000	54	1000	5000	400	15
23-50	70	154	172	69	2700	56	1000	5000	—	15
51+	70	154	172	69	2400	56	1000	5000	—	15
FEMALES										
11-14	44	97	155	62	2400	44	800	4000	400	10
15-18	54	119	162	65	2100	48	800	4000	400	11
19-22	58	128	162	65	2100	46	800	4000	400	12
23-50	58	128	162	65	2000	46	800	4000	—	12
51+	58	128	162	65	1800	46	800	4000	—	12
PREGNANT					+300	+30	1000	5000	400	15
LACTATING					+500	+20	1200	6000	400	15

1 The allowances are intended to provide for individual variations among most normal persons as they live in the United States under usual environmental stresses. Diets should be based on a variety of common foods in order to provide other nutrients for which human requirements have been less well defined.

2 Kilojoules (KJ)=4.2 x kcal.

3 Retinol equivalents.

4 Assumed to be all as retinol in milk during the first six months of life. All subsequent intakes are assumed to be one-half as retinol and one-half as β-carotene when calculated from international units. As retinol equivalents, three-fourths are as retinol and one-fourth as β-carotene.

5 Total vitamin E activity, estimated to be 80 percent as ɑ-tocopherol and 20 percent other tocopherols.

RECOMMENDED DAILY DIETARY ALLOWANCES (*cont.*)

	(years) From Up to	Weight (kg)	Weight (lbs)	Height (cm)	Height (in)	Energy (kcal)	Protein (g)	Minerals Calcium (mg)	Phosphorus (mg)	Iodine (µg)	Iron (mg)	Magnesium (mg)	Zinc (mg)
INFANTS	0.0-0.5	6	14	60	24	kg x 117	kg x 2.2	360	240	35	10	60	3
	0.5-1.0	9	20	71	28	kg x 108	kg x 2.0	540	400	45	15	70	5
CHILDREN	1-3	13	28	86	34	1300	23	800	800	60	15	150	10
	4-6	20	44	110	44	1800	30	800	800	80	10	200	10
	7-10	30	66	135	54	2400	36	800	800	110	10	250	10

MALES	11-14	44	97	158	63	2800	44	1200	1200	130	18	350	15
	15-18	61	134	172	69	3000	54	1200	1200	150	18	400	15
	19-22	67	147	172	69	3000	54	800	800	140	10	350	15
	23-50	70	154	172	69	2700	56	800	800	130	10	350	15
	51+	70	154	172	69	2400	56	800	800	110	10	350	15
FEMALES	11-14	44	97	155	62	2400	44	1200	1200	115	18	300	15
	15-18	54	119	162	65	2100	48	1200	1200	115	18	300	15
	19-22	58	128	162	65	2100	46	800	800	100	18	300	15
	23-50	58	128	162	65	2000	46	800	800	100	18	300	15
	51+	58	128	162	65	1800	46	800	800	80	10	300	15
PREGNANT						+300	+30	1200	1200	125	18+[8]	450	20
LACTATING						+500	+20	1200	1200	150	18	450	25

[8] This increased requirement cannot be met by ordinary diets; therefore, the use of supplemental iron is recommended.

RECOMMENDED DAILY DIETARY ALLOWANCES (cont.)

Water-Soluble Vitamins

	From Up to (years)	Weight (kg)	Weight (lbs)	Height (cm)	Height (in)	Energy (kcal)	Protein (g)	Ascorbic Acid (mg)	Folacin[6] (µg)	Niacin[7] (mg)	Riboflavin (mg)	Thiamin (mg)	Vitamin B6 (mg)	Vitamin B12 (µg)
INFANTS	0.0-0.5	6	14	60	24	kg x 117	kg x 2.2	35	50	5	0.4	0.3	0.3	0.3
	0.5-1.0	9	20	71	28	kg x 108	kg x 2.0	35	50	8	0.6	0.5	0.4	0.3
CHILDREN	1-3	13	28	86	34	1300	23	40	100	9	0.8	0.7	0.6	1.0
	4-6	20	44	110	44	1800	30	40	200	12	1.1	0.9	0.9	1.5
	7-10	30	66	135	54	2400	36	40	300	16	1.2	1.2	1.2	2.0

MALES	11-14	44	97	158	63	2800	44	45	400	18	1.5	1.4	1.6	3.0
	15-18	61	134	172	69	3000	54	45	400	20	1.8	1.5	1.8	3.0
	19-22	67	147	172	69	3000	54	45	400	20	1.8	1.5	2.0	3.0
	23-50	70	154	172	69	2700	56	45	400	18	1.6	1.4	2.0	3.0
	51+	70	154	172	69	2400	56	45	400	16	1.5	1.2	2.0	3.0
FEMALES	11-14	44	97	155	62	2400	44	45	400	16	1.3	1.2	1.6	3.0
	15-18	54	119	162	65	2100	48	45	400	14	1.4	1.1	2.0	3.0
	19-22	58	128	162	65	2100	46	45	400	14	1.4	1.1	2.0	3.0
	23-50	58	128	162	65	2000	46	45	400	13	1.2	1.0	2.0	3.0
	51+	58	128	162	65	1800	46	45	400	12	1.1	1.0	2.0	3.0
PREGNANT						+300	+30	60	800	+2	+0.3	+0.3	2.5	4.0
LACTATING						+500	+20	60	600	+4	+0.5	+0.3	2.5	4.0

* The folacin allowances refer to dietary sources as determined by *Lactobacillus casei* assay. Pure forms of folacin may be effective in doses less than one-fourth of the RDA.

' Although allowances are expressed as niacin, it is recognized that on the average 1 mg of niacin is derived from each 60 mg of dietary tryptophan.

trip. Any person in reasonably good health should
be able to get along on the barest of diets for several
days without difficulty. In fact, most survival experts
agree that food should not be a consideration for at
least two weeks in the survival emergency. Although
food is important for the mental and emotional attitude of the victims, most of them can live quite
well for two weeks on stored body fat. Such a schedule
might actually do a few of us a lot of good!

If the outing lasts a couple of weeks or more, the
nutritional intake becomes a great deal more important. It is then that the body's ability to restore
itself and maintain a high level of energy is seriously
affected by a proper (or improper) diet. Sufficient
water and other liquids, of course, must be taken
from the very beginning; normal functions are quickly
disrupted by a lack of liquids. Again, approved survival techniques recognize water as one of the two
most critical elements in the wilderness emergency.

To fully understand the need for the three essential
fuels—protein, fats, and carbohydrates—it is necessary to know their functions within the body. Although the descriptions provided here are quite
simplified, they will adequately explain the need for
these food elements in the wilderness environment.

Proteins may be derived from either plant or animal foods, but plant proteins are seldom complete.
A vegetarian diet dictates the use of several plant
protein sources to insure a complete and useful sub-
stance. Proteins are composed of carbon, hydrogen,

Vitamins and minerals can be supplied by taking one of the supplemental vitamin pills along.

oxygen, nitrogen, phosphorus, sulfur, and iron—which make up the greater part of plant and animal tissue. These basic elements combine to form amino acids, the building blocks of proteins—a complete protein being one that contains all the essential amino acids, which are necessary for growth and maintenance of body weight.

Proteins are a source of heat and energy for the body; they are essential for growth, the building of new tissue, and the repair of injured or broken-down tissue. They form an integral part of the protoplasm of every body cell. Proteins are oxidized by the body, thus liberating heat. One gram is said to supply about 4 calories of internal heat, and 0.65 grams of protein will compensate for the wear of about 1 kilogram of body tissue or body weight under normal conditions. That amount is the minimum requirement as a basal protein level when the body is at rest. Obviously, the strenuous activity of camping and hiking requires many times that level.

Carbohydrates are organic compounds in which hydrogen and oxygen are found in the same ratio as in water. Glucose and sucrose (sugars) are typical carbohydrates, but the group also includes the noncrystalline destrins and starches.

Carbohydrate foods contain such combinations of carbon with hydrogen and oxygen as sugar, starch, and cellulose. Carbohydrates, principally starches, provide a major source of calories in the average diet and are especially important to the hiker during times of increased activity.

Fats are generally unrecognized as the stalwarts of the outdoor diet. Fats have a high caloric value, yielding 9.3 calories per gram, as compared to 4.0 calories per gram in carbohydrates and 4.1 calories per gram in protein. The average diet of 3,000 calories per day should take between 30 to 40 percent of its caloric value from fats. Despite modern advertising, which tells us fats should be avoided, this figure is particularly important to the outdoor diet. In addition to their nutritive values, fats improve the taste and odor of foods, provide a feeling of satiety, are absorbed slowly (prolonging their nutritive effects) and because of their high caloric content are especially important to the high calorie diet required by the active hiker and camper.

As we examine the trail menu and calculate the correct foods to provide the essential proteins, carbohydrates, and fats, we must be careful to recognize the value of the latter. The science of dietetics has outlined the following important contributions of fat to the body: (1) Fats serve as a high source of energy; (2) Subcutaneous fats form an insulating layer which prevents loss of heat; (3) Fats act to support and protect certain organs such as the eye and kidney; (4) They provide a concentrated reserve of food; (5) They provide essential acids necessary for normal growth; (6) In conjunction with carbohydrates fats serve as protein sparers; (7) Fats are an important constituent of cell structure.

Fats are certainly no more important, in this rather specialized diet, than are carbohydrates and proteins, but neither are they less important. From a simple, practical point of view, Proteins are necessary for keeping the body in good working order, Carbohydrates provide a quick source of energy and the reserves for longer-lasting power, and Fats are necessary for long-term energy needs. To be efficient in the field, a person should include a good balance of all three in his diet. As previously pointed out, this balance is not especially critical on the short trip, but it is enormously important on the longer outing. For the quick overnight trip or a normal weekend on the trail, taste and convenience may be allowed to dictate the menu.

When hikers are planning the meal list for a short trip, they must still be concerned with the quick replenishment of energy. These quick energy demands will vary, of course, according to the usual routine of the party members. Those who work at largely seden-

tary jobs, with little need for a generous store of energy in their daily lives, will find their strength levels diminishing quite rapidly on the trail. Those accustomed to vigorous physical activity in their normal routine will find their energy levels staying fairly constant while hiking. These factors should be considered in planning the trail menu, even over the shorter periods of the weekend outing.

The normally office-bound hiker must augment his diet in camp with a number of quick trail snacks containing both sugars and fats to meet the increased immediate demands for energy. The sugars provide a short burst which peaks and falls in a matter of minutes. The fats (and some proteins) are absorbed more slowly, providing a longer lasting source of power that is utilized as it is needed.

Ideally, three major meals each day will give the hiker this residual energy reserve, and the trail snacks will be available when the demands increase or the energy reserves weaken. The trail snack is obviously an important part of the meal planning process. It is so valuable to the overall enjoyment of the adventure that we cannot afford to take a casual approach to it.

The most universally recognized and widely used trail snack is a combination of familiar ingredients known as "gorp". Although the variations in this finger-food are practically endless, it is usually built around a generous supply of shelled peanuts. In fact, the name "gorp" is really an acronym for "Good Old Reliable Peanuts!" Long before the nutritive value of the peanut was known, hikers all over the country recognized that a handful of gorp along the trail helped them work harder and feel better. Science has since merely confirmed what a lot of people already knew.

In most cases, gorp consists of about half peanuts and the remainder a haphazard mixture of candy, raisins, dried fruits, and other exotic foods. Clinically

Gorp (Good Old Reliable Peanuts) is the universal finger-food of the backpacker. It supplies immense amounts of energy and calories on the normal outing.

examined, it is a great answer to the nutritional needs of the trail. The peanuts are quite high in protein, fair in carbohydrates, and an excellent source of readily available fats. The candy and fruits contain various carbohydrates—in the form of sugars—which release energy quickly. Both foods are good in caloric value.

As we examine the value of a typical gorp recipe, we can also see the ways the three building blocks of energy apply to our regular menu. As the balance between protein, carbohydrates, and fats can be adjusted in the gorp, so can they be adjusted in the camp dinner. It is simply a matter of understanding the food requirements of the party and including the items that will meet them.

As we examine the gorp ingredients, we will also look at the caloric content of each. As daily calorie requirements are discussed a little later, the totals included in the gorp will be considered a part of the daily intake. The gorp, beside providing some very real momentary benefits along the trail, may constitute from 10 to 20 percent of the variable calorie requirement for the whole day.

Here are the figures for three typical gorp items in nutritional terms; all the figures are based on a 100-gram sample (about ½ cup).

Ingredient (100-gram sample)	Protein (grams)	Carbohydrate (grams)	Fats (grams)	Energy (calories)
Peanuts, cocktail	26.0	18.8	49.8	585
Raisins	7.7	56.9	32.3	520
Chocolate Drops	2.5	77.4	0.2	289

As we can see, peanuts are the best protein source of the three and are high in calories and fats. They lack the essential carbohydrates, but the raisins, although low in protein, are high in calories and fats, and are excellent sources of carbohydrates. The candy is highest in carbohydrates, moderate in calories, but contains almost no protein or fat. By mixing them equally, we can see the resultant nutritional combination.

Gorp (100-gram total)	Protein (grams)	Carbohydrate (grams)	Fats (grams)	Energy (calories)
Equal parts	12.0	51.0	27.4	464.6

This is a good mix, but it can be improved by changing the ratio of ingredients. Let's examine a gorp recipe that includes 50 grams of peanuts, and 25 grams each of raisins and chocolate candy drops.

Gorp (100-gram total)	Protein (grams)	Carbohydrate (grams)	Fats (grams)	Energy (calories)
Peanuts 50%				
Raisins 25%	15.5	47.97	33.0	494.75
Chocolate 25%				

Although this mix is slightly lower in carbohydrates, and thus provides a bit less instant energy, it is significantly higher in both protein and fats. It would be a wise choice on a longer trip, since the increased protein and fat content allows greater satiety and a better source of residual energy.

Finally, let's look at a gorp recipe specially compounded for an afternoon or a overnight trip with a lot of physical activity. Here the requirement will be for a high-recovery food with a lot of carbohydrate and lesser amounts of protein and fats. The caloric content is not terribly important on this short trip.

Gorp (100-gram total)	Protein (grams)	Carbohydrate (grams)	Fats (grams)	Energy (calories)
Peanuts 25%				
Raisins 25%	9.67	57.6	20.62	420.75
Chocolate 50%				

This mixture answers the needs by providing a bit less protein and fat, but gives about 18 percent more carbohydrates than the previous recipe. The calories are substantially lower, but that wasn't much of a consideration in this case.

These comparisons are especially valuable for the reasonably experienced hiker who has a particular need for increased protein or an added shot of quick energy along the way. With a little trial-and-error practice, it is fairly easy to custom tailor the gorp mix to any individual need. People with special diet problems, of course, should consult their physician before experimenting with the food they take. A diabetic would probably use whole grains or something else in place of the fruits and candy, while a hypoglycemia case would likely require fewer peanuts and much more sugar and other carbohydrates in their gorp mixture.

The amount of food required during the increased activity of hiking and camping has long been a subject of dispute. Some authorities insist that there need be little, if any, change from the food intake during normal periods. That might be a fine theoretical point, but it is hardly a practical approach to hiking and backpacking. I wonder whether these experts ever leave their desks and notebooks long enough to feel *real* hunger. The vast majority of physicians and nutritionists—particularly those involved in military research or the demands of professional athletics— agree that there should be an increase in caloric intake that roughly corresponds to the increase in physical exertion. The need for more energy-producing elements increases as the period of heightened activity is extended. There are no cut-and-dried figures available, but the military and athletic researchers have accepted an arbitrary level of 4,000-5,000 calories per day as an intelligent starting point. Other factors may cause that figure to vary considerably, depending on the individual and the activity. Cold weather, for example, may require the expenditure of half the body's fuel just to provide internal heat. If a winter hike of moderate difficulty is planned, an intake of 6,000 calories or more is not unreasonable. A warm weather stroll on a relatively flat trail might require no more than the 3,000-calorie norm outlined by the RDA.

At the risk of offending the entire dietetic community, I suggest that the experience of hiking produces so many variables—and individual metabolism can be so different—that no formulae exist for calculating the necessary number of calories that are right for a given person under differing circumstances. The only proper guideline for such a determination is how you feel at the time, how able you are to respond to the demands placed on your muscles under certain conditions. It is a matter of the most personal nature, to be discovered only through experience. If you eat enough to be comfortable without distending your own little tummy, and you greet each day with the enthusiasm to continue, you are probably achieving the proper balance between proteins, carbohydrates, and fats. If those conditions exist, your calorie intake is just about right, whether you are hiking or not!

Perhaps the only way any of us will ever find exactly how much we need on the trail is to go out there and find out. From my own experience, I know that two members of a trail party—under identical conditions—will vary enormously in their food requirements. On any trip, the energy needs of any person will vary from day to day to such an extent that the daily food list is an approximation at best. After a few days, a few trips, each of us gets to know just how hungry we can expect to be, just how much food will be required to keep us fit and happy. That is the basis on which food planning is done. The 4,000-5,000 calorie figure is a basic guideline for the novice, from which the individual needs will be discovered.

Over the years I have seen the differences the trail has on my own group. My wife, after a long day on the trail, may eat only enough to keep a lethargic sparrow alive, while my 16-year-old son will devour a pile of food that would strangle a killer whale—and then spend the rest of the evening munching on the gunnysack of gorp he's carried along! A large hiking party of such growing young men, incidentally, should never be left alone with the pack animals before suppertime; they might develop a taste for roast mule!

I began this chapter by observing that the science of nutrition is an exact and detailed one, then spent the rest of this essay carefully destroying that statement. From a practical point of view, that is precisely the situation with regard to the hiker and backpacker. I really hope that the food sciences spend a little more of their time studying the somewhat paradoxical state of the hiker, but I doubt that it will happen soon. In the meantime, our meals should be guided by a working knowledge of basic nutrition, some lively experimentation over the backpack stove, and the ability to recognize health and vigor within ourselves. Armed with these few tools, the mechanics of selecting, preparing, and eating the right foods along the way will be possible, if not perfect.

I have a hunch that when science finally gets around to us hikers, that is just what they'll tell us to do anyway!

3

Cooking Equipment

Across the trails of this country on any summer
afternoon, you are apt to see just about every imagin-
able combination of pots, pans, rusty buckets, and
tin cans disguised as cooking gear—and most of
them, surprisingly enough, are doing an admirable
job. It wasn't very long ago that an acceptable cook
outfit consisted of a large iron skillet, a couple of
coffee cans, and a timeworn spatula. These few items
were all that was needed to prepare the rather un-
eventful meals that passed for standard trail fare.
Composed mostly of flour and bacon grease, yesterday's grub probably wouldn't have tasted a bit
different had it been cooked in a hollow rock or a GI

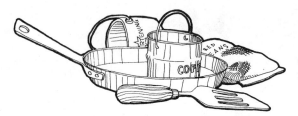

The old-time cookset consisted of little more than a cast-iron skillet and a couple of coffee cans. Simplicity is still to be desired, but we need not be quite that rustic.

helmet, so the cook kit really wasn't all that important.

Today's trailside chef has a chance to create some really fine gourmet treats for his hiking party, ranging from a hearty Denver omelette at breakfast to Shrimp Amandine in the evening. Fortunately for all of us, trail cookery has emerged from the barbaric ages and entered a new era of sophisticated enjoyment.

Even the most involved of supper meals has become a lot easier because of the imaginative food combinations at the local supermarket and a fascinating collection of new edibles at the outfitter's shop. Most of these new dinner treats could probably be cooked reasonably well in the old skillet-and-can rigs, but they seem to work (and taste) considerably better when prepared with the more efficient modern utensils. A modern portable pantry, by the way, is neither expensive nor difficult to accumulate. Except for the backpack stove, none of the essentials of good camp cookery costs more than a few dollars.

The backpack stove, the heart of any well-conceived cook kit, has grown enormously in both popularity and importance in this day of mass migration to the summer woods, and for a very good reason: the

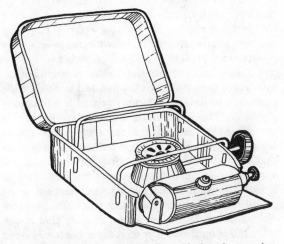

A typical-design white gas stove has a fuel tank, vaporizer-burner, and sturdy carrying case in a single unit.

building of a fire for every campsite meal is no longer possible in many places—and ethically wrong in most others.

For several decades the American wilderness has been host to a growing throng of hikers and backpackers who have trod its more popular areas into a quagmire. It isn't a question of careless or unthinking people heading afield to do the greatest damage possible, but simply of too many people in too small a space in too short a time. Along the easier trails and the nearer lakes it is impossible to find enough fuel to satisfy even a handful of campfires, much less the hundreds or thousands that would be needed without the portable stoves. We are necessarily changing our own relationship with the wilderness—in a very positive way—and the backpack stove is perhaps the most important contribution to this changing ethic.

In years past we have chopped and hacked at the landscape until there is simply no fuel at all in many places, and those who insist on a daily fire are quickly denuding the rest. No one can dispute the charm and comfort of a flickering fire, but we must all realize that the day of the indiscriminate fire has long disappeared. We must be satisfied with our more efficient stoves, perhaps allowing ourselves a small campfire in those rare instances when fuel and conditions permit. We must adopt an ethic that recognizes the open fire as a special favor bestowed upon us by a benevolent nature, not as a birthright we've earned from our pioneering forebears.

Deciding when a campfire is suitable is something of a dilemma in the modern wilderness. In most instances we would really like to have one, and it seems fairly easy to rationalize the existing factors on that basis. The concerned and prudent hiker, however, will let environmental considerations outweigh his personal desires, and the fire will usually be left unlit.

Of course, when weather conditions go sour and the party is up against a tough night in wet gear, the fire becomes very necessary. In those rare circumstances, the environmental factors must be waived in favor of human safety. Anyone who has ever come to grips with hypothermia knows only too well the value of shelter and a warming fire. Some forest administrators are in favor of designating the open fire as a survival technique, to be used only in cases of dire emergency. It may come to that, but for the present there are still a lot of times when a fire is morally and practically permissible.

The true test for deciding whether or not to build a fire involves two questions: (1) Is there plenty of waste wood around for fuel? (2) Can it be removed without changing the character of the wilderness? If both conditions hold, go ahead and have a fire. Keep it as small as practicable, fueling it only as needed and enjoying it thoroughly. As a cooking medium, the open fire is not as efficient as the backpack stove, but there is a certain enjoyment to cooking over an open fire that cannot be duplicated with our specialized equipment. If you have a fire, make sure the

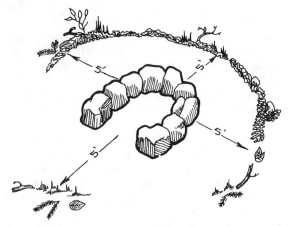

If a fire will be built, clear all burnable material down to mineral soil at least 5 feet from the fire in any direction.

firepit is eradicated before you break camp, and that you never expose the wilderness to wild fire. For the most part, camp cooking will be done on the backpack stoves carried by the party.

In choosing this central piece of gear one must consider fuel type, weight of stove and fuel, amount of heat produced, and under what conditions the stove will be used. Some stoves, for example, are not efficient at very high altitudes, while others are difficult to use in wind or rain. Look the stock over carefully before plunking your hard-earned rubles down for a new camp stove.

Most backpack stoves are fueled by either white gas, kerosene, or pressurized propane or butane. We will examine each of these types in detail, but the prospective buyer must determine the availability of the specific fuel in his area before choosing. At this point we will mention a fourth fuel type, alcohol, that is favored by a few mountaineers because of its extreme light weight, but we'll dismiss it for general hiking. These very small alcohol models are just not practical for the family hiker or backpacker who will cook for several people.

Alcohol, white gas, and kerosene are usually available in just about any part of the country and none of the three is particularly expensive. The pressurized cannisters for propane or butane stoves are a little more difficult to find in some areas, but are becoming easier to locate as the stoves become more popular.

White gas stoves are possibly the most widespread in current usage, largely because these efficient burners were developed before the other types. Among the advantages of white gas systems are their lighter weight, high heat output, the universal availability of their fuel, and the fact that spilled fuel evaporates quickly. On the negative side, the fuel is extremely volatile, the stove needs priming before it efficiently vaporizes the fuel, it is difficult to light or use in wind, and it must be insulated from snow to operate properly. White gas is flammable to the point of being explosive—a factor to consider when choosing a stove.

Kerosene stoves are another excellent device for the backpacker, with many new designs on the market that have significantly reduced the weight of older models. The advantages of kerosene include: readily available fuel, pump pressure systems that reduce priming time, high heat output, and low-volatile fuel that will not ignite readily if spilled. The disadvantages are the relatively greater weight (compared to white gas models), the priming period required on some stoves, the fact that spilled fuel will not evaporate quickly, and the difficulty of operation in wind. The pressure system stoves seem to work quite well at high elevations, and the fuel is less explosive than white gas.

The various pressurized propane or butane stoves are a good choice for the hiker who seldom spends more than three days on the trail or in camp, since the spare cannisters are heavy and awkward. Disposal of expended cannisters can be a problem; they simply must be carried back out. One of the chief advantages of the pressure cannister stove is the instant heat output—no priming or pre-burn time required. In addition, there is no chance for fuel spillage. The disadvantages of the propane system are serious enough that it must be carefully weighed against white gas or kerosene types. The fuel cost is quite high and cartridges are not always available in every area. As previously noted, fuel cannisters are heavy and present a disposal problem. The fuel must be kept above freezing, total output is lower than either

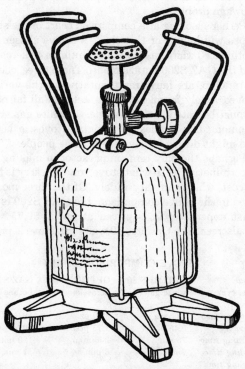

A typical propane stove is a reliable source of immediate heat, but is relatively heavy, presents a disposal problem, and has somewhat lower maximum heat output than gas or kerosene.

white gas or kerosene, and many cannisters cannot
be removed until they are empty—which presents a
stowage problem.

Perhaps looking at a comparison chart of the stove
types will help. For this chart we have chosen the
Optimus 80 white gas stove, the Optimus 48 kerosene,
and the GAZ S200 butane model. These three, chosen
at random, are fairly representative of the various
stoves widely found in the markets. In all fairness,
it must be noted that the model 80 white gas stove
is among the smallest of popular stoves; a larger
one might do the job better for some people.

Perhaps the only remaining factor in making the
determination as to what stove you will carry is that
of cost, which can vary widely. Of the three models
used in the above comparison, the GAZ S200 is the
least expensive. It is priced at about $9.75 with
windscreen. The Optimus 80 white gas stove is priced

STOVE COMPARISON CHART

Model	OPTIMUS 80	OPTIMUS 48	GAZ S200
Fuel type	white gas	kerosene	butane
Weight (without fuel)	18.5 oz.	39.0 oz.	19.0 oz.*
Capacity	0.45 pts.	1.75 pts.	10.50 pts.**
Burning time	75 min.	240 min.	180 min.
Boiling time	7 min.	6 min.	11 min.
Boiling time (at 14,000 ft.)	8-11 min.	7-12 min.	12-15 min.

*with windscreen
**equivalent

at around $13 in most shops, while the Optimus 48 kerosene model sells for around $21 (1976 prices). Larger white gas stoves, comparable in fuel capacity and burning time with the Optimus 48 kerosene, may run as much as $30.

The use of these three stoves for comparison is just intended as a guide; it is not a recommendation of any given stove—or fuel type—over another. Any well-equipped outfitter will likely carry three or four different brands in as many as two dozen models. The final choice will be dictated by the needs and desires of the person who will be using it.

The vast majority of backpackers choose white gas, simply for the ease of operation and light weight. In the past couple of years we have seen a lot more use of kerosene, largely because it is safer. A few hikers pick the butane models because they are relatively inexpensive and childishly simple to operate. There is something to be said for each of them, and the final choice will be purely personal.

Once this monumental decision has been made there is one more important step: learn the stove intimately! Begin with the instruction book that comes with it. You should become familiar with all the little tubes and valves and orifices that make it work. Learn to disassemble it, clean it, and put it all back together. Learn the proper method of filling, priming, lighting, and pressurizing your stove *before* you find yourself trying to fix dinner on a dark and windy night. Be particularly careful when learning to fill and light the stove, since nearly all the common accidents occur during one of these processes. Don't ever try to refill a hot stove. It's a lot better to delay dinner a half-hour while your stove cools than to risk a potentially tragic accident because of hunger or impatience. Learn to use your new acquisition properly, keep it clean, and it will return years of safe, dependable service.

With the stove chosen and packed away, it is time to start assembling the cook kit—the half-dozen utensils that will become the core of your culinary reputation along the trail. Somewhere among the incredible array of pots and pans on the market is the handful that is just right for you and your appetite. It is just a matter of finding them.

The most basic cooking tool for the average backpacker is his frying pan, the modern descendant of the cast-iron skillet. That omnipresent device was the key to every meal in the old-timer's trail camp, and it is no less important to the modern adventurer. With the skillet you can fry eggs or hotcakes, bake bannock bread, simmer a trail stew, brown up some fresh trout, or kill spiders! It will do just about everything in camp except brew coffee—and in a pinch has been known to do that.

There are many different kinds of frying pans on the market today, and just about any one except the newfangled electric ones will do nicely for the hiker. (Even they aren't too bad, but the extension cord is murder!) Specialized frying pans with slick coatings and folding handles are available at the mountain shops, but the average pan from the hardware or discount store will work pretty well. The special backpack pans are a bit more adaptable for our purposes, particularly since they are lighter and easier to carry, but the chief difference is the folding or removable handle. Beyond that, big deal!

A 9½-inch pan is probably the best bet for most hikers, although the smaller 8-inch size is fine if you don't cook for more than two people. Spun aluminum pans are very lightweight, although the life span is shorter than that of the stainless steel types. Aluminum frying pans are generally less expensive than the stainless, but both are usually available with Teflon® coatings and will provide good service. You'll find both types without the stick-proof coatings, of

A modern backpack frypan features a folding handle and an easy-to-clean Teflon® coating. Such pans are relatively inexpensive.

course, but you'd be well advised to choose the Teflon® coated pans; cleanup is tough enough as it is. In either case, nylon spatulas are a good choice since they are light and tough, yet flexible enough to stand the occasional bending they get in the pack.

Even though the old skillet-and-coffee-can outfit is largely a relic of our rough-and-tumble past, a startling number of hikers get along very nicely with about the same setup. The old coffee cans, fitted with coat hanger handles, tend to burn through rather quickly at the most inopportune moments, but they can be replaced cheaply and easily. Better grade cooking pots, available at reasonable cost, seem to wear pretty well and are simple to keep clean. Generally known as "billies," a set of three heavy gauge aluminum pots (in 1-, 2-, and 3-quart size) will cost less than $10. These are usually fitted with sturdy handles and good lids that can double as plates or even frying pans. The whole set weighs less than 2 pounds, and the stove will sometimes nest inside the smallest pot, making a light and compact unit.

The hiker on a threadbare budget might forego the nesting set in favor of two or three graduated cans to which he has fitted handles—and will get along famously. A fixed-handled, coated frying pan can usually be purchased at the local Salvation Army store for a few cents, and a usable spatula and spoon can be found at the same source. With an expenditure of less than $2, an efficient, if somewhat rustic, cook kit can be assembled that will serve all the demands

A nesting set of cooking pots gives great flexibility to the cook and simplifies packing and carrying chores. The lids double as plates or utility cooking utensils.

of the trail. The commercial outfits might look better and be a little more flexible, but it is possible to tailor the cook kit to your own circumstances and budget. The production camp pots are a lot easier to clean than the square-edged cans—a factor to consider from the standpoint of cleanliness and sanitation.

With the large frying pan, 1-, 2-, and 3-quart cooking pots, and a spatula all assembled, about the only other item needed will be a small covered tea kettle. The smallest of the standard cooking pots can be used for tea or coffee water, but the little tea kettle is more than a luxury; it heats quickly, keeps the water warm while other things are cooking, and is

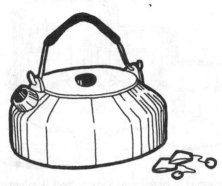

The tiny tea kettle may not be a necessity along the trail, but it is a comfortable addition to the cook kit.

really handy for the quick trail lunch. The pot of water can make tea and soup quickly during the abbreviated stop, without your having to unpack the rest of the gear.

Finishing off the portable pantry will be the few items of individual eating equipment: cups, plates, and silverware. There are all kinds of aluminum plates, flat or sectioned, on the market at reasonable cost. Some plastic variations are also around that are perhaps a little more comfortable to use, since they tend to keep the food warm a bit longer. By the same token a plastic cup keeps the chocolate hot longer without risk of burning the lips, a constant threat with metal cups. The exception, of course, is the efficient "sierra" cup, an almost universal fixture along the trails. I have an old reliable sierra swinging from my pack on every trip, and it makes a great dipper for a cool creekside drink or my luncheon soup. Still, I carry a couple of thick plastic cups in my cook kit for mixing foods and drinking my morning coffee or hot broth in the evening camp. I find them more comfortable and efficient than any metal cup I've ever used.

Before you choose the plates you will carry, consider the use of a bowl instead. A few years back I started carrying thick plastic bowls instead of plates, and have become a firm advocate of their use. I take the colorful kind that margarine comes in. They are cheap, virtually unbreakable, and surprisingly efficient. Hotcakes and eggs are just fine in bowls, and the sloppy stuff like stew and chili handle a lot better. Moreover, the thick plastic will keep food warm much longer than a metal plate, make the meal more appetizing, and never give a tinny taste to the food. From the standpoint of weight, the bowls are actually a trifle lighter than aluminum plates. Their compact size and shape allow them to fit better in the pack.

Around camp, a couple of plastic bowls are a heck of a lot more efficient than the combination of plates and mixing pans. I can reconstitute my eggs in a bowl, pour them in the frying pan, and, while they cook, rinse the bowl. After I eat the eggs from that same bowl, the whole process is repeated with hotcake batter—and breakfast is finished with only one bowl and one pan to wash. I admit to being basically lazy, but the whole thing just seems more efficient. (By the way, I usually mix and eat with chopsticks, which are also easy to clean. Talk about lazy!)

The basic cook kit, in all its simplicity, is a darned handy and efficient collection of elements. A typical kit would break down like this:

Frypan and handle	12 oz.
Spatula, nylon	1 oz.
Nesting pots with lids	1 lb. 8 oz.
Tea kettle, 4-cup	7 oz.
Plastic bowls, 3	6 oz.
Cups, 3	6 oz.
Silverware, etc.	4 oz.
TOTAL	3 lbs. 12 oz.

Thick plastic bowls are good for many parties since they keep food warm longer than metal plates. They are lightweight and inexpensive, but cleaning them can be a chore.

This isn't an unreasonable weight for two people, although it includes an extra bowl and cup for mixing, unexpected guests, and other situations. One of the three nesting pots could as easily be used, reducing the overall weight a little.

There are many interesting innovations in cooking gear worth considering, particularly for those who hike a lot or take long trips. These departures from standard equipment are valuable for producing new taste and excitement over the long haul, utilizing more economical foods, or simply adding a little novelty to the trailside fare.

PRESSURE COOKER

Recently developed lightweight cookers are much more efficient than the old home-canning devices, and have proven themselves very important at high elevations. With pressure valves and perforated separators, the new cookers weigh a shade under three pounds and hold a full four quarts, making them ideal for larger groups. More important, they cut cooking time by half at 10,000 feet or more, producing better food and conserving fuel. Before the development of the pressure unit, a lot of skyline hikers found they couldn't cook foods such as rice or beans. It is a bit disheartening to cook rice for an hour and have it come out tasting like a handful of B B's. The backpack stove gets them perking in short order.

THE WOK

This ancient Chinese utensil is really nothing more
than a heavy steel bowl that concentrates the heat
in one spot. The wok has long been recognized for
producing outstanding flavors with an economy of
ingredients. Averaging about three pounds, the wok
works beautifully over the backpack stove. It is designed primarily for cooking substantial rice and
noodle dishes, and lends itself well to large hiking
parties. The wok can be considered a piece of community gear on the hike, so the rest of the cooking
gear can be distributed around the group, lessening
the load on the cook.

DUTCH OVEN

A thoroughly impractical device for the backpacker,
the Dutch oven is best suited for trailhead or campground dinners near the car. It is much too heavy for
backpacking, but far too valuable to overlook completely. It cannot be used over a backpack stove—it
requires much more heat than can be produced by
the single burner unit. Several recipes are included
later in this book that utilize the Dutch oven, and it
is a beautiful way to start or end a hiking adventure.

THE TOASTITE

Another novel form of cooking utensil, strictly
limited to the campground because of size and weight,

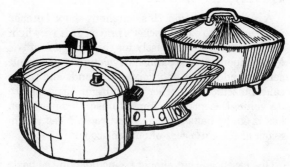

Among the more useful novelty cooking tools are the pressure cooker, the Chinese wok, and the Dutch oven. The latter is strictly a car-camp item since it weighs eight or ten pounds.

the toastite will produce some of the neatest cooked sandwiches you've ever tasted. The heavier ingredients required for the toastite are also poor candidates for backpack cookery.

THE REFLECTOR OVEN

This is one of the oldest baking devices on earth, yet it still works surprisingly well if you have an open fire. Most hikers probably won't use the reflector because of the need for a fire and the heavier ingredients, but it is fun to know and use when circumstances allow. A variation is the baking pan oven, which requires a little more equipment but is easy to use.

THE BACKPACK OVEN

A recent innovation, this doughnut-shaped utensil is the answer to a backpacker's prayer. It is very light and was designed expressly for the backpack stove. More important, the parallel development of a whole series of add-water-only mixes for bundt and coffee cakes, biscuits, and other baked items has added to its value. Deceptively simple to use, this new oven has brought baked biscuits and roast meat within reach of the clumsiest of outdoor cooks.

One essential that should be included in the basic cook kit, although it is usually considered an accessory, is aluminum foil in generous supply. The uses of foil are numerous, and the results are often just as good as any rigid pot can produce, sometimes a lot

Reflector oven, toastite, and the new backpack oven.

better! Imagination seems the only limit to foil's utility around the camp. Much of the foil can be saved and re-used, but those pieces to which food has adhered can be a disposal problem. Used foil is not burnable, and must be carried back out with all the other non-combustible trash generated by the party. For heaven's sake, Don't leave it littering the campsite, and Don't bury it to save the few ounces on the outbound trip. Before long the whole wilderness would be little more than an unsanitary landfill!

Another genre of outdoor cookery has overstepped the bounds of civilization into the genuinely barbaric. Loosely called "rustic cooking," it is just that: cob-rough and ash-dirty. Probably no one would give it a second thought if it weren't so darned much fun!

The most elementary method of rustic cooking is to toss something in the fire until it sizzles, retrieve it with a stick, and eat it. Fortunately, not many foods lend themselves to such treatment, so we don't have to experiment much, which is probably better for our collective digestion. If you happen to have a hind-quarter of ox in camp it might work, but it leaves dehydrated eggs a bit the worse for wear.

Try impaling your dinner on a sharp stick and holding it in the flames. This ancient method is great for wieners and marshmallows, but not at all good for lasagne. There was a folksy way of preparing potatoes and ears of corn by wrapping them in mud and nestling them in the coals of the fire, but it got difficult to tell where the mud quit and the potato started!

Carrying bags should be fashioned to custom-fit the cook kit. They keep everything together and prevent the rest of the gear from getting sooty or soiled.

Substitute foil and it works just fine, if you happen to have potatoes and corn along in the backpack.

Finally, there is the parlor trick school of outdoor cookery in which eggs are boiled in paper cups or fried on hot rocks. These novelties will work if the food responds to such treatment, but they are nothing more than tricks. As a departure from the ordinary they are fun to fool with, but don't ever let them be a substitute for the tried-and-true techniques of trail cookery. When your hotcake batter becomes only slightly more palatable than the rock you cook it on, you'll wish you'd brought the frying pan!

Gimmicks and gadgets aside, the majority of outdoor cooking will be performed over the backpack stove on the basic frying pan and in two or three pots. I have purposely omitted the open-fire grill and the hatchet as essentials of camp cookery. I honestly believe that the day of the open-fire has passed; we must learn to live with the more efficient—and environmentally superior—backpack stove.

With a little practice and time the cook kit will become a familiar old friend. Virtually every concoction in the gastronomic inventory can be prepared with it, the flavors can be as varied and exciting as the imagination of the cook, and the nutritional value can be kept as high as the trail demands. Your gear may be as simple or elaborate as you wish, but it will eventually boil down to a frying pan or two and some nesting pots or cans. After all, it's what goes in 'em that counts!

4

Planning

No single facet of the outdoor experience is so sadly neglected as the pre-trip plan, yet it is doubtful that any other phase of a trip contributes more directly to its success. With a proper plan to guide the party, there is no reason for anyone's going hungry, sleeping on the hard ground, or facing a difficult survival situation. Without a decent trip plan, these disasters can be the rule, rather than the exception.

The trip plan—whether for an afternoon walk or a week in the mountains—must be accomplished with careful consideration long before the party jumps into the brush. It is done in four separate but closely related stages, each somewhat dependent on the others. The four planning phases are: (a) trip planning, (b) equipment planning, (c) menu planning, and (d) health and safety planning. Each is just as important as the other and none can be underestimated or overlooked. Obviously, a great many ill-planned trips turn out all right, with the participants blundering along under the protection of dumb luck. More often than not, however, the party that becomes the object of a rescue mission is one that failed adequately to plan its outing.

The planning stages, beside being critical to the outcome of the adventure, can also be a heck of a lot of fun. It is during this period that anticipation becomes real, and the party begins whetting its appetite for the fun and experience that lies ahead. When I consider the many fine hours my friends and I have spent poring over our maps and jotting down notes (whether we took the trip or not), I find it difficult to believe that so many people deny themselves this part of the experience.

Since this book is about trail cooking and associated arts, we will touch only briefly on the other three stages of trip planning. By examining the overall plan we will see how the relationship between the other planning elements and the menu can contribute to the final success of the trip.

The trip plan is a general timetable for the party, a listing of destinations and intermediate goals, and a close examination of the route the party will follow. This stage usually begins when someone decides it's time for another ramble into the wilderness, calls a few friends who might enjoy going along, and ar-

ranges a meeting to start planning. By the time the
group actually gets together there are three or four
potential trips that seem reasonable, so a weeding out
process begins. One or two of the possibilities eliminate themselves for one reason or another, one looks
pretty good, and one fairly shouts to be taken. With
that decision made, the hard and fast planning begins.

A topographic map of the area is the prime essential
for this part of the plan. On it the group will mark
its ultimate destination, overnight stops, and an
estimate of the time each leg of the journey will require. One can see from the topographic data just how
difficult each section of the route will be, then decide
where to enter the wilderness, through which areas
it will be the most fun to pass, and where to come
out. Knowing the time factors involved it is an easy
matter to jot down a rough timetable that will tell
where the party should be at any given time, and
where and when the trip should be over. After this
important information is collected, it should be copied
and given to someone who can notify authorities if
the party fails to return reasonably near its schedule.
This information, similar to the flight plan filed by
an aircraft pilot, will give searchers the vital details
they need to effect a successful rescue should things
go amiss. Most search-and-rescue agencies agree that
this single step—filing a trip plan with a friend who
can notify authorities—would eliminate most of the
unsuccessful rescues that occur each season. Too
many hikers have perished in the wilderness while

searchers were combing the woods many miles away, simply because nobody left behind an accurate trip plan.

With the timetable finished and a copy given to a buddy, the second stage can be covered: the equipment plan. This stage lets the party decide what basic or specialized equipment to take along. The usual gear would include sleeping bags, shelters, backpacks, and clean socks. The party would then check to be sure it had the ten essentials required on any trip. To refresh our memories, the ten essentials include:

1. Extra food
2. Extra clothing
3. First aid kit
4. Knife
5. Flashlight
6. Sunglasses
7. Waterproof matches
8. Firestarter
9. Compass
10. Map

The communal and specialized gear would be chosen on the basis of where the trip is planned, how long the stay, and the activities planned. This might include photo or fishing gear, technical climbing equipment, or butterfly nets.

With the equipment list finished, it is time to think about the food supplies, menu, and cooking gear that will be included. It is important that this phase be given extra attention since the mental attitude, physical stamina, and outright enjoyment of the party depends so much on wholesome food and an attractive diet.

First, determine which meals will be eaten on the trail on which days. Consult the trip plan for this information and make a list. For our example, we will plan a three-day weekend outing. Friday breakfast will be eaten before we leave, so it needn't be on the list. Sunday dinner will be eaten at a restaurant on the way home, so leave it off as well. The basic meal plan will include only the actual food to be consumed on the trail.

FRIDAY	SATURDAY	SUNDAY
Trail snacks	Breakfast	Breakfast
Lunch	Trail snacks	Trail snacks
Trail snacks	Lunch	Lunch
Dinner	Trail snacks	Trail snacks
	Dinner	

Actually, seven meals will be eaten during the trail and camp portion of this weekend, plus enough gorp or other snacks for six in-between stops. These snacks are essential to the food list, since they provide quick energy, a high calorie count, and a source of sustaining energy. On the average, a hiker would probably need about 8 or more ounces of gorp each day, which would provide from 600 to 1,000 of his daily 4,000-5,000 calorie intake. As you can see, the snacks are really a big part of the trail diet, constituting as much as 25 percent of the total food input. We simply can't afford a casual approach to trail snacks!

With the meals roughed in, the actual menu can be developed and the actual dishes that will be prepared put on the list. This stage is usually the subject of some healthy debate among the hikers, one of whom might be a meat-and-potatoes type, and another partial to tossed salads, french onion soup, and fruit cocktail. The finished menu ought to include something for everyone. After the arguing and arm waving, a typical day's menu might look like this:

SATURDAY

Breakfast 7 A.M.	*Lunch Noon*	*Dinner 6 P.M.*
Scrambled eggs	Vegetable soup	Eggs and ham
Hash browns	Pilot bread	Savory rice
Hotcakes and	Hot chocolate	Vegetable medley
honey	Trail cookies	Applesauce
Coffee		Fudge brownies
Orange drink		Coffee or tea

Snack 10 A.M.	*Snack 3 P.M.*
Pilot bread	Gorp
Peanut butter	Limeade
Gorp and Tea	

This sample menu was chosen from a list of freeze-dried and dehydrated foods available at almost any outdoor store. It would be a bit expensive, so many hikers would probably substitute some supermarket foods for some of the trail specialties. In following

chapters we will discuss ways of designing an entire
menu of lower-cost supermarket foods while main-
taining high food values and light packs. Don't overlook the value of the excellent freeze-dried foods from
a flavor and nutrition standpoint, even though they
tend to be a bit expensive.

The sample menu looks pretty good from here, and
chances are most hikers wouldn't give it another
thought. They'd buy the necessary foods, stuff them
in the pack, and enjoy the heck out of the weekend.
But since we are concerned with energy and food
value as well as good taste, let's examine the menu
from that aspect. Referring to the earlier chapter on
basic nutrition, this food list should provide about
4,000 to 5,000 calories, a good balance between protein, carbohydrates, and fats; and include about one-
fourth of the calories as fats, to provide long-lasting
energy. To be considered a well-planned trailside
meal, it must do at least that much for us.

Item	Serving Size	Energy (Calories)	Protein (Grams)	Carbo. (Grams)	Fats (Grams)
Scrambled eggs*	3.5 oz.	171	10.9	3.9	17.0
Hash browns*	4 oz.	240	3.0	39.0	8.0
Hotcakes and honey	7 oz.	350	7.0	78.4	1.0
Orange drink	8 oz.	120	—	30.0	—
Vegetable soup	8 oz.	128	3.6	21.2	3.4
Pilot bread	4 oz.	439	9.2	70.6	13.1
Pilot bread (snack)	2 oz.	220	4.6	35.3	6.5
Peanut butter	1 oz.	150	5.0	5.5	13.0
Gorp	4 oz.	464	12.0	51.0	27.4

Item	Serving Size	Energy (Calories)	Protein (Grams)	Carbo. (Grams)	Fats (Grams)
Hot chocolate	8 oz.	117	3.0	25.0	—
Trail cookies	2 oz.	282	4.0	37.0	13.0
Eggs and ham	5 oz.	275	17.7	5.9	20.0
Savory rice	12 oz.	335	16.0	58.3	4.2
Vegetable medley	2 oz.	69	2.0	14.6	—
Applesauce	4 oz.	119	—	28.0	—
Fudge brownies	3 oz.	412	6.0	43.0	27.0
Gorp	4 oz.	464	12.0	51.0	27.4
Limeade	8 oz.	120	—	30.0	—
NUTRITIONAL TOTALS		4475	116.0	627.7	181.0

*Cooked in ½ oz. margarine.

If nothing more than taste and keeping our tummies full mattered, this menu would do the job nicely. But from our nutritional examination, we find it also satisfies the demands of the trail. It provides a daily intake of 4,475 calories, the mid-range of hiking requirements. It has an excellent balance of nutrients, providing about twice the RDA of protein—an important factor during periods of increased physical activity. Finally, it furnishes more than 25 percent of the calories as fat, the best source of long term energy production. All things considered, there is little more we could ask of a trail menu. Coupled with the fact that the foods are attractive and tasty, this day of eating should be an integral part of the enjoyment of the trip, provided Charlie doesn't burn the rice or sit on the brownies!

Achieving the proper balance isn't as difficult as it might seem, and there is no reason for any hiking party to sit down and list the nutritional elements of every meal. If there is enough to eat, including something from each of the four food groups every day, we will achieve the good balance we are looking for. The four groups: meat and fish, dairy products, cereals and grains, and fruits and vegetables, are not too hard to fit into the trail diet. A few years ago both meats and dairy products were pretty unmanageable in the woods, but present developments in freeze-drying and dehydration have made them readily available.

After the menu has been carefully planned and each party member has his share of favorites included, another package of food must be put together. Strictly an emergency source of energy, a survival ration should be chosen and packed. One of the ten essentials, this extra food should be carried separately from the regular meals. The emergency ration should be easy to prepare, include food and hot drink, and be especially high in carbohydrates and fat. Protein is not particularly important in the survival ration, but a high calorie count is.

One of the neatest combinations I've seen in emergency rations is a package of enriched egg noodles, a packet of dehydrated stew vegetables, and two envelopes of beef gravy mix. Weighing less than a pound, it can provide several abbreviated meals in an emergency. Each of these small meals has a rela-

tively high carbohydrate-fat count and they taste fine. To prepare, just put some of the noodles in boiling water, add a few vegetables, and toss in a pinch of the gravy mix. It is best not to drain the dish, but to drink the liquid instead. The water contains more than enough nutrients to make it valuable, while the gravy mix makes it taste rich and hearty.

Under survival conditions this emergency packet can give the party a great boost in spirit while it is providing the essential nourishment to continue. In a lot of cases the psychological effect of the meal is more important than the calories. Most people can survive nicely for several days or weeks with absolutely nothing to eat, but their mental attitude is vastly improved with even one small meal each day.

The survival ration should first be wrapped in a large square of foil (which can be used as a rustic cooking pot if necessary) and then enclosed in a waterproof

The emergency ration should be easy to cook, lightweight,
and safe to store. It should provide hot food and drink
and be high in carbohydrates, fats, and calories.

plastic bag. Thus protected, the emergency food will
last almost indefinitely and be in little danger of
damage inside the pack.

With the meal list now complete—including the
emergency rations—make up a shopping list. This is
another overlooked step. The average party will often
simply take menu in hand and head for the supermarket. By trying to buy directly from the meal
schedule they will invariably get too much of one
thing and not enough of another. The menu will then
have to be adjusted in the field, which usually brings
up some kind of problem. If you have plenty of hotcake mix but no syrup or honey, it becomes drudgery
to choke those dry devils down. Hash browns and
scrambled eggs without salt are a bit tasteless, too.

Salt and honey are little things that don't really affect the nutritional value of the food, but they can seriously alter the social life of the camp chef!

Translate the food requirements into a complete list, including accessories and condiments, and head for the neighborhood supermarket. If nothing else, the food list will keep you from impulse buying, a practice that usually costs more than necessary and adds a pound to an already heavy pack. If the meal planning has been efficient those impulse items will end up back at home, having made the round trip on your back. If you multiply the ounces of unnecessary food you carry by the number of steps you take, it adds up to a lot of nonproductive work.

One small detail remains before this stage of the plan is complete: the choice of cooking gear. With a basic kit already assembled it really isn't a big deal, but the size of the party will influence this selection. If six or eight hikers are taking to the trail together, one backpack stove just isn't going to be sufficient. Neither are one frying pan and one set of pots going to feed the mob adequately. Breakfast would be a three-hour affair ending just in time for lunch.

A larger party can be fed a lot more efficiently if the cooking is divided into units of two or four. In a party of eight, for example, there would be two cooks, two complete cook kits, and, in effect, two kitchens operating simultaneously. A really expert trail chef can prepare large meals without much fuss, but there aren't that many experts around. Some of the best-planned larger groups I've seen did their meal planning, preparation, and packing in groups of two. In that manner, everyone's dinner was ready at the same time and the entire group sat around thoroughly enjoying the food and the company. A family, of course, usually eats as a group, but they've had a lot of practice. For the casual, loose-knit group that often comprises a hiking party, the buddy system is quite efficient.

If the menu calls for specially prepared meals, be sure to carry the necessary implements to do the job. If the party will be enjoying any of the many fine Chinese dishes on the trail, for instance, it is best not to forget the wok. On the other hand, if none of the foods will be fried, the frying pan is just excess baggage.

With the meals completely planned, right down to the condiments and correct utensils, the group can turn its attention to the final planning phase: health and safety. The gear will always include a first aid kit (remember the ten essentials?) and should anticipate special hazards along the way. In some areas a snakebite kit, sunburn cream, and poison ivy lotion are essential; in others they would be just extra junk to carry. A few areas would require extra raingear and fungicide foot powders to prepare for the special hazards of the rain forests. Whatever the problem, advance health and safety planning would have recognized the need for the right equipment. Party members with individual medical problems should carry the proper medication and brief their companions on how to administer it in an emergency.

Part of the health plan should include a method of keeping clean, particularly if the trip is extended over several days. Many groups carry a small plastic basin for an occasional sponge bath. One enterprising group brought along a plastic spray bottle of about a quart capacity. Retiring to a secluded spot, each person would take a close-up shower with the pump-and-spray bottle. However it is done, a little bath is nice for removing the buildup of insect repellent and perspiration that accumulates along the trail. This

practice also keeps the party from taking on the character of a flock of gamey sheep!

It is impossible to overemphasize the value of pre-trip planning in the four essential areas. Whenever a wilderness outing is a spectacular success, good planning played an important part in the adventure. By the same token, the trip that disintegrates into bedlam was ill-planned, if planned at all. The time spent in planning can be part of the fun of the trip, in addition to assuring a memorable wilderness experience.

5

Supermarket Foods

When a backpacker starts choosing the food that will be taken on a particular trip, he is sometimes amazed at the sheer bulk of the supplies the party will need for a week or ten days. If he should just go back in time some forty years and see the piles of stores necessary then, he'd shoulder his pack gladly, knowing his logistics problems were just a drop in the bucket by comparison.

One of the oldest guidebooks in my library has a grub list for a two-man, ten-day excursion into the woods. Among other things, the provisions include 20 pounds of meat, 8 pounds of ham, 4 pounds of bacon, 4 pounds of boiled ham, 20 pounds of potatoes, 8 pounds of flour, roughly 18 pounds of canned juice,

and 1 pound of salt. The total load for these two healthy appetites was 254 pounds, nearly 13 pounds per person each day!

By 1971 the weight estimates for a hiking party had been reduced to around 4.5 pounds per day, and this figure is for a menu actually designed for a horse camp. But even with that drastic reduction in the grub list, the outdoor camp was certainly no place for

anyone weak of limb or short of breath. Even if those
unreasonable weights wouldn't stop a hiker today,
the cost of such a food list would keep most of us out
of the battle. The development of modern freeze-drying and dehydration techniques has reduced both the
weight and cost of the fundamental foods we must
carry.

The current hiker can choose strictly freeze-dried
trail foods (fully covered in the next chapter) for his
camp fare, and get along on no more than 30 ounces
of provisions a day. By selecting only highly dried
foods that can be reconstituted with water the reduction can be even greater. To prepare this special food
we need only stir in a little boiling water; it will quickly regain size and flavor. Of course, it will cost around
80¢ an ounce to live so conveniently. The freeze-dried
specialties are among the most costly foods on the
market, largely because of the extended processes
required to make them as light as they are.

So, the average hiker of moderate means is faced
with something of a dilemma. He hasn't the physical
ability to carry up to five pounds of food for each day
he would spend in the wilderness nor the financial
resources to pay up to $75 per week for his meals on
the trail. But the picture is not as grim as it might
appear; the answer is as near as the corner supermarket.

Giant food processing corporations, feverishly
competing for the food dollar by making life easier
for the housewife, have inadvertently given the hiker

and backpacker a wealth of low-cost, lightweight foods that fit perfectly into the trail menu. Many of the mass-produced grocery items on the shelves are processed in exactly the same manner as the more expensive trail foods at the outfitter's shop. By shopping carefully and combining the two food sources, most hikers can outfit their party with a good balance between food weight and cost. For example, only the label and the package differ between a 21¢ packet of onion soup at the supermarket and the 68¢ backpack brand. On the other hand, bacon-flavored textured vegetable protein at the mountain shop costs about 13¢ an ounce, while the supermarket gets about 48¢ an ounce for the same product to sprinkle on our baked potatoes. Careful shopping does not necessarily mean buying at the grocery store. It means getting to know the various food resources and using the one that suits us best.

The neighborhood supermarket variety of food will be adequate for almost every hiking requirement. These mass-produced foods are somewhat heavier than mountain shop trail food, but the cost reduction more than compensates for the added weight. From a purely practical point of view the mass-market foods will satisfy the needs of all but the most unusual hiking circumstances. The ultralight freeze-drieds have an important place in the outdoor menu, but if they are used in combination with the common foods an acceptable cost-to-weight ratio can be achieved by nearly everyone.

It is not necessary to sacrifice either taste or nutrition in order to use the less expensive forms of prepared and packaged foods. There are hundreds of suitable foods on the shelves of any well-stocked market; their use is limited only by the imagination of the chef. By taking advantage of the tremendous variety of common foods that fit in the canvas cupboard, even a fledgling hiker should be able to provide his party with a delightful and varied menu. There is no need to settle into a dreadful routine of stew-every-day-on-the-trail.

Recent food and drug regulations require nutritional labelling on nearly all foods. This policy is perhaps a greater boon to the hiker than to the housewife for whom they were designed. While the family cook is understandably concerned about the day-to-day maintenance of health, the backpacker has some very specific nutritional requirements to meet if he is to function with any degree of efficiency. Vitamins and minerals are not really a great concern in the foreign environment of the trail; we must concentrate on the energy components and calories that reach far beyond average daily needs. The nutrition labels, when they finally become universal, will assist significantly in choosing the everyday foods that will meet the rigid demands of the trail.

Nobody should be surprised that the meat-and-potatoes appetites of the hiker can be met at the corner grocery. For years we have been accustomed to dehydrated potato, noodle, macaroni and cheese dinners, and powdered soup mixes. The surprise comes when an experienced camp chef whips up a Shrimp Creole or a frosted chocolate cake over the camp stove. Fresh fudge brownies and butterscotch pudding are not at all difficult; the ingredients and techniques already exist for producing exotic camp foods from mostly grocery store foods. Better still, such treats can be whipped up for just a few cents a serving.

A lot of rice and stew has been consumed by otherwise experienced hikers who wish like crazy they could turn out better trail meals, yet these people are as skeptical as anyone else when told that the products already exist to lift them out of their culinary rut. The point can best be made by listing a few of the commonly available foods that lend themselves to trail cookery. This shopping guide was compiled by a simple walk through a national chain supermarket with a pad and pencil. Almost anyone would be able to add many items we overlooked.

NOTE: *Many of these foods may require milk or egg for mixing. Consult the recipe section for specific directions.*

Breakfast Items

Pancake mix—A staple; choose the "add water only" varieties.
Biscuit mix—Several types need only water to mix.

Corn meal—Check the recipe section for ideas.

Breakfast bars—New on the market; better for snacks than breakfast.

Breakfast tarts—Toast these for a minute over the stove.

Instant breakfast—Powdered milk must be added; check recipe section.

Cold cereals—Pretty fragile, but the 1 oz. boxes are OK.

Cooked cereals—Cook quickly, need powdered milk plus sugar or honey.

Hash browns—Delicious, light, easy to cook.

Honey—Good substitute for sugar or syrup.

Syrup—Heavy, mostly packaged in glass; transfer to plastic tubes.

Lunch Items

Cheese spread—In squeeze tubes, no refrigeration needed.

Cheese food—Foil-wrapped loaves need no refrigeration.

Peanut butter—Valuable for protein, needs repackaging for hiking.

Sardines—Tin becomes a disposal problem.

Tuna, shrimp, etc.—Tin becomes a disposal problem.

Potted meats—Aluminum cans; carry them back out.

Vienna sausage—Not much value for their weight, but tasty.

Canned meats—Good for shorter trips, but quite heavy.

Snack crackers—Many flavors and high carbohydrates; fragile.

Saltines—Extremely fragile, lots of calories.

Graham crackers—High calories but very hard to pack without damage.

Pilot bread—Very high calorie content, fairly sturdy.

Fig bars—Tasty, durable, lots of calories and carbohydrates.

Assorted cookies—Some pack well, good food value.

Snack pack fruits—Fairly heavy, disposal of can a problem.

Snack pack puddings—Fairly heavy, disposal of can a problem.

Canned fruits—Very heavy, major disposal problem.

Soups

Condensed or canned—Much too heavy for long trips, disposal problem.

Instant mixes—Perfect!

Cup-of-soup® mix—Not as efficient as the larger mixes, but acceptable.

Bouillon cubes—Good for hot drinks and to add to recipes.

Cup of noodles—Fine flavor, no cooking required.

Split peas, dry—Good, but long cooking period needed.

Lentils, dry—Same as above. Both have high calorie
values.
Flavored rice mixes—Excellent.
Rice, dry—A staple, but requires long cooking period.
Instant rice—Cooks faster, more efficient for hiking.
Helper® dinners—Can be super if vegetable protein
is added; see recipes.
Flavored noodle mixes—Absolutely great for hikers.
Macaroni and cheese—Complete dinners in a light
package.
Noodles, dry—A basic for many excellent recipes.
Macaroni, dry—A basic for many excellent recipes.
Spaghetti, dry—A basic for many excellent recipes.

Potatoes

Scalloped—Good choice, see recipe section for instructions.
Au gratin—Good choice, see recipe section for instructions.
Mashed—Most require only water to mix, but check
recipe section.

Snack Items

Raisins—Doesn't everybody?
Dried fruits—Dozens of varieties and uses.
Nuts—For just about everything.
Beef jerky—High protein, but expensive.
Smoked sausage—OK, but watch for mold or spoil-
age after 2 days.

Obviously this kind of a list could go on forever, with perhaps a couple hundred different items included. A lot of canned products like chili or pork and beans will be useful for overnight trips or short weekends, while things like fresh fruits, cheeses, and lunch meats can be carried for the first day's lunch. In all but the hottest weather these items are reasonable for a whole weekend, but care should be exercised if they are used.

There are nearly a hundred different drink mixes on the market today, all of which require only water (sometimes sugar) to reconstitute. Many hot chocolate mixes come in little packets just right for backpacking, as do instant tea and instant coffee. If only somebody could succeed in making a powdered martini, practically every drink known to mankind would be available for the backpack!

Now that we have established that there are almost no limits to the kinds of food the grocery store makes available to the trailside chef, let's qualify what we have learned. Modern packaging is really fine for the kitchen, I suppose, but it falls short of meeting the demands of the backpack. Some of the packaging of cookies and crackers, for example, is just too flimsy to be of any value on the trail. Repacking this kind of food is merely a matter of providing a reasonably sturdy container. Plastic freezer containers seem to work nicely, are very inexpensive, and their weight is minimal. The 1-quart size can be used to pack crackers, cookies, a bag of cold cereal, and several other items at once, making a compact unit.

Some of the standard packages are unacceptable for other reasons. They may be too heavy, breakable, or both. Sometimes we can find honey, syrup, mustard, or other such items in plastic squeeze bottles, but more often we must repack them in more suitable containers. Many outdoor stores handle refillable plastic tubes that are the perfect answer, but small squeeze bottles from the dime store or even plastic prescription bottles can be pressed into service if necessary. The prescription bottles can be obtained at nominal cost from almost any pharmacy, and are absolutely ideal for peanut butter, margarine, sugar, instant coffee, and like commodities. The plastic drug bottles come in a wide range of sizes, will fit into any nook or cranny in the pack, and can take one heck of a beating.

Other of the supermarket foods must be repackaged for an entirely different reason: the size is just not practical for the backpack party. The food industry has become so obsessed with family-size packaging that it is difficult for a hiker slogging around in the woods to utilize their food efficiently. Even the common tin of condensed soup makes 21 ounces when cooked according to directions (a trifle more than a normal individual could, or would, comfortably eat). This family-packaging concept is abundantly clear to any single person who has wrestled with four-to-a-package pork chops.

One of the handiest new food products to come along in years, at least for the backpacker, is the Helper® dinner, to which you must add a pound of

Supermarket foods may be adapted to the backpack by preplanning, weighing on a diet scale, and packaging according to individual need along the trail.

hamburger or other meat. Packaged in boxes serving five, they just won't work for a couple of hikers unless repacked in useful quantities. A description of the repackaging of a helper dinner will illustrate the techniques for utilizing most supermarket foods. The necessary paraphernalia consists of a cheap diet scale, a few plastic bags, and a roll of masking tape.

Assuming we are going to adapt a beef stew mix to the trail, open the five-serving box and set it aside. (Don't discard it; it has the cooking directions you'll need in the field.) Usually there will be two envelopes inside, one of dehydrated vegetables and another of potatoes. The vegetable packet contains the flavorings and spices.

The two packages need merely be weighed and divided into equal units. If the trip is imminent, put half the potatoes and half the vegetable mix into one plastic bag. Next, put a 2-ounce package of beef-flavored textured vegetable protein into the bag, along with the cooking directions you've jotted down on a slip of paper. Seal the whole package with masking tape and write "Beef Stew" on the tape. In this way you have provided a neat package that contains 2½ servings (just right for the healthier appetites on the trail) and needs only boiling water to prepare.

There is one other source of backpack food that we shouldn't overlook, particularly when it comes to condiments and spices, and that's the local Big Buster hamburger store, which has zillions of little packages of salt, pepper, sugar, mustard, ketchup, and heaven knows what else. These single-serving packets were developed for the fast-food industry, but can usually be purchased in small quantities for the retail outlet. Of course if you are really cheap, just pocket a few on every visit for a super grumbleburger, and by spring you should have enough for the season. You'll even find small plastic tubs of jams and jellies if you drop in at breakfast time. A little conscientious tight-waddery will pay big dividends when hiking season rolls around.

When designing a week's menu around the supermarket foods, it may be a bit difficult to determine if you have provided enough calories or hit the right balance among essential nutrients. Until the nutrition labels become widespread, it is a problem we will have to live with. There are sources of nutritional data for commonly used foods, of course, and if you are interested you may want to check at the local library. The bible of the nutritional community is U.S. Department of Agriculture Handbook No. 8, entitled "Composition of Foods". It provides unbelievably complete nutritional data on 2,483 common (and not so common) edible foods presented in a format that can be comprehended by the most hopeless dolt. If the library has never heard of it, you may order a copy from the Superintendent of Documents, U.S. Government Printing Office, Washington, D.C. 20402. It costs $1.50 and is an excellent source of information for anyone who cares what he puts in his body.

The garden variety of supermarket foods will probably supply most of what a party would like on the trail, and could undoubtedly be used exclusively, if that's what we want. Still, the variety and flavor of the specially processed trail foods should be considered by those who hike more than a couple of days a year. They are amazingly compact and convenient, have been designed to meet the high nutritional demands of the trail, and are really a lot of fun. Even if many hikers will use them only occasionally, it is good to know what they are and how to use them. For most of us, the supermarket foods will be the staple, but the special trail foods are a resource we will use to great advantage.

6

Backpack Foods

It was only a few years ago that backpacking exploded into the national phenomenon that it is today. During the second century of America's development the wilderness was shrinking faster than most people realized, but urban sprawl had not yet reached today's absurd proportions. The wilderness was more to be feared and avoided than explored and enjoyed. The pressure of an advancing society had not yet touched so many lives. Then, in the last two decades, the exodus to the wilderness began.

This turn of events coincided almost exactly with sweeping changes in the food-processing industry, a situation viewed with mixed emotions by many who choose the woods as a temporary way of life. The new

convenience foods proliferated on the market, but
their individual values were diminished by hybridi-
zation, mass processing, and nutritional strangula-
tion in the name of food preservation. To these brave
new foods were added all sorts of questionable chemical agents to improve flavor or retard spoilage. We
escaped to the woods, but we brought some of the
worst of our ills with us!

The science of food processing improved, however,
along with much of our other technology, and soon a
new food form appeared, designed specifically for
the hiker and backpacker. Based on a largely natural
dehydration and freezing process, the trail foods
were a vast improvement over earlier lightweights.
They preserved more of the flavor and nutrients
while allowing us the ease and convenience of greatly
reduced weight. Although backpack foods still have
a way to go, the demands of several million occa-

sional hikers are being met remarkably well by this emerging industry. The freeze-dried foods could not be correctly called health foods, but there is no reason they should be. They have been designed and produced to fill a narrowly specialized need—and they do that very efficiently.

If there is one area of the backpack-food industry that could stand massive improvement, it is packaging. Many firms who furnish preselected complete meals have encased their offerings in as many as a dozen different kinds of packages, all enclosed in a larger packet. No doubt this is a result of the current state of the art, but it could stand some hard study and improvement. Still, the packaging is better suited to our needs than the family-oriented supermarket monstrosities we examined in the last chapter.

There are currently several large national concerns devoted entirely to the production of freeze-dried and dehydrated backpack foods, and an astonishing number of smaller, regional firms producing trail foods. It would be completely unfair to try and generalize about the industry in either food quality and taste or packaging. Some products are better than others; we simply have to find the brands and products that suit us best.

Nearly all the special food firms that serve the outdoor public have extensive lists of their products and prices, most of which can be had by dropping them a note. Some of the larger firms regularly supply food catalogs to the various outfitters and shops that handle their products, so copies may be picked up while shopping for other items.

The quality of today's specialized trail food is actually a lot better than one would suspect. Most producers start with the very best raw ingredients and process them in the best known ways. In recent years, many of the larger manufacturers have taken a very responsible attitude toward the quality and nutritional value of their products. There are federal standards for these foods, food-quality minimums and consumer-protection regulations. It is to their credit that most major manufacturers far exceed the minimums set by the food and drug regulations.

At present there is a nutritional labelling program being implemented in the United States by the federal Food and Drug Administration. Not all the trail foods are yet so marked, but eventually they will be. Because of the very long shelf life of most of these foods and the relatively lower demand for them (as compared to supermarket varieties), it may be some time before all trail food packages contain the required nutritional information. In point of fact, not all the smaller producers have yet *established* the nutritional values of their products. When the present stocks are gone and all the packages have this information on them, meal planning will be a bit simpler for most hikers. Without consulting a bunch of technical tables, we will be able to know just how many calories, how much protein, and what nutrients we are getting with each serving.

There is one serious drawback to the general use of freeze-dried trail foods for most of us: the cost. Because of the high quality of the initial raw materials and the extensive processes required to prepare them, they hit the market at what appear to be outrageous prices. In truth, however, they represent a reasonable value in terms of taste and nourishment. It would be terribly costly to use these special foods to the exclusion of all others, and fortunately the supermarket foods listed in the previous chapter can take care of most menu requirements. Using trail foods in combination with standard grocery items is one way of achieving high nutritive value at a moderate cost.

A number of current hiking books have listings of various food manufacturers and addresses at which food lists can be obtained, but most of these lists are out of date. The industry is growing at such a rate that many firms move into larger quarters in between mail deliveries! The most reliable source of addresses for the freeze-dried food companies is the local mountain shop that supplies the foods, or one of the popular hiking magazines. Many of the larger mail-order camping suppliers list these foods in their regular catalogs, a fine source of information for those who can't regularly visit a store. One of the nation's largest outdoor outfitters, Recreational Equipment Inc. (REI), of Seattle, WA. and Berkeley, CA., has an excellent listing of trail foods, including a few items packed expressly for them at quite reasonable cost.

Most of the country's larger processors are also represented, including Mountain House, Tea Kettle Foods, Rich-Moor, Wilson's Freeze Dried Foods, Seidel's Trail Packets, and Dri-Lite. Without specifically recommending one supplier over another, I note that the REI catalog lists over 175 different trail foods and combinations and that it is free. The address is 1525 11th Ave., Seattle, WA. 98122. I *will* specifically recommend the textured vegetable protein packaged for REI. Available in both beef and ham flavor, a 2-ounce package weighs nearly ½ pound after it is reconstituted. Many of the recipes in this book call for this vegetable protein product, and it costs just 25¢ per 2-ounce packet.

The overall food value of most of the freeze-dried and other trail foods is high. Many of these foods are packaged without preservatives or other chemicals, but it is necessary to check each item individually to be sure. In a lot of cases, of course, the food could not be safely processed without the addition of a chemical preservative.

The following list of food values is for a specific brand, but the values are for the most part comparable to those of other brands. The nutritional data in this list was furnished by Rich-Moor Corp., P.O. Box 2728, Van Nuys, CA 91404, to whom we are indebted for sharing the results of this nutritional research. The food items are listed by the Rich-Moor package name. Other brands with the same item designation may vary in their nutritional value, but a spot analysis of similar food combinations by other producers has yielded essentially the same values. Note that all nutritional data are for serving samples prepared according to package directions.

Product Name	Serving Size	Energy (Calories)	Carbo. (Grams)	Protein (Grams)	Fat (Grams)
Breakfast Items					
Orange juice drink	8 oz.	147	32.9	0.53	0.57
Oatmeal and milk	9 oz.	300	49.0	17.0	5.0
Scrambled eggs	3.5 oz.	121	3.9	10.9	7.0
Sierra coffee cake	5 oz.	290	62.2	5.4	10.8
Buttermilk pancakes	4-5 oz.	318	34.7	4.7	5.1
Blueberry pancakes	4-5 oz.	283	60.0	7.0	1.0
Maple syrup	2 oz.	175	44.0	—	—
Sunrise cereal	2.75 oz.	324	49.0	17.0	7.0
Biscuit bar	4 oz.	312	51.0	8.0	9.0
Natural nuggets	3 oz.	324	49.0	17.0	8.0
Astro eggs	4.5 oz.	171	9.0	10.9	9.0
Eggs w/imit. bacon	5 oz.	170	3.9	10.9	7.0
Western omelette	5 oz.	207	6.0	13.0	7.6
Hash browns	4 oz.	170	39.0	3.0	—
Main Courses					
Veg. beef stew	11 oz.	204	27.2	12.0	5.3
Chicken stew	11 oz.	223	23.0	20.5	5.4
Lasagna/meatballs	12 oz.	386	50.7	22.5	10.2
Beef stroganoff	12 oz.	369	50.0	18.2	10.7
Tuna noodle	12 oz.	337	47.0	24.8	5.5
Cheese romanoff/ham	12 oz.	386	46.8	18.6	13.8
Savory rice	12 oz.	335	58.3	16.0	4.2
Eggs 'n ham	5 oz.	275	5.9	17.7	20.0
Chicken à la king	14 oz.	340	53.5	17.3	6.4
Shrimp creole	10.5 oz.	301	40.0	13.0	10.0
Lasagna/It. sauce	10.5 oz.	315	41.0	18.0	8.0

Product Name	Serving Size	Energy (Calories)	Carbo. (Grams)	Protein (Grams)	Fat (Grams)
Spaghetti/Tomato sauce	10.5 oz.	281	49.0	15.0	2.0
Chili noodle	10 oz.	269	40.0	28.0	—
Turkey supreme	10.5 oz.	309	38.0	20.0	8.0
Meatballs w/ Pot. and gravy	14 oz.	311	38.4	15.2	10.8
Macaroni/cheese	12 oz.	344	53.8	14.6	7.8
Chili Mac. w/beef	11.5 oz.	307	50.2	16.3	4.6
Chicken rice	9.5 oz.	285	45.2	13.9	5.2
Beverages					
Orange drink	8 oz.	120	30.0	—	—
Lemon lime	8 oz.	120	30.0	—	—
Grape	8 oz.	120	30.0	—	—
Fruit punch	8 oz.	120	30.0	—	—
Chocolate shake	9 oz.	273	54.0	12.0	1.4
Sweet milk cocoa	8 oz.	117	25.0	3.0	—
Vegetables					
Potatoes O'Brien	4 oz.	164	37.0	3.0	—
Hash browns	4 oz.	170	39.0	3.0	—
Mashed potatoes	8 oz.	147	32.0	4.0	—
Carrot slices	2.5 oz.	69	14.6	2.0	0.3
Corn, frz/dry	1.5 oz.	59	12.1	1.5	0.5
Peas, frz/dry	2 oz.	46	8.3	2.8	0.2
Green beans	2 oz.	27	3.3	0.9	0.1
Peas and carrots	2.5 oz.	44	9.0	1.0	—
Spreads					
Cheddar cheese	2 oz.	136	5.6	8.6	8.8
Swiss cheese	2 oz.	124	11.0	7.0	5.0
Peanut butter	1.5 oz.	128	7.8	9.4	6.7
Berry jelly	1.5 oz.	69	17.5	1.0	—

Product Name	Serving Size	Energy (Calories)	Carbo. (Grams)	Protein (Grams)	Fat (Grams)
Fruits and Desserts					
Applesauce	4.5 oz.	119	28.0	—	—
Fruit cocktail	5 oz.	145	34.5	—	—
Lemon pie	6.5 oz.	280	63.0	3.0	2.0
Rasp. cobbler	6.5 oz.	301	68.0	3.0	2.0
Blue. cobbler	6.5 oz.	326	66.0	1.0	6.4
Pin. cheesecake	5.5 oz.	287	14.0	7.0	2.0
Fudge brownies	4 oz.	412	43.0	6.0	27.0
Apple compote	5 oz.	139	33.0	—	—
Choc. pudding	5 oz.	148	31.0	5.0	1.0
Btsctch pudding	5 oz.	124	26.4	3.9	0.4
Banana cr. pudding	5 oz.	149	31.0	5.0	—
Cherry pie	6.5 oz.	307	69.0	3.0	2.0
Trail Snacks					
Trail brunch OM	2.75 oz.	330	53.0	5.0	11.0
Trail brunch choc	2.75 oz.	352	57.0	5.0	12.0
Apple slices	1 oz.	100	26.0	—	—
Ice cream frz/dry	.6 oz.	159	26.8	2.8	4.5
Trail cookies	2 oz.	282	37.0	4.0	13.0
Trail cookies PB	2 oz.	268	38.0	6.0	11.0
Apple chips	1 oz.	106	26.0	—	—
Banana chips	1 oz.	163	25.0	1.0	—
Pilot biscuits	2.5 oz.	181	34.0	6.0	2.0
Meats					
Bacon bars	3 oz.	400	3.0	30.1	29.7
Meat bars	3 oz.	478	—	40.4	35.2
Beef roll	1 oz.	47	—	8.0	1.0
Beef jerky	1.6 oz.	94	—	16.0	4.0

The foregoing is a cross section of the hundreds of specialized foods presently available to the backpacker. Undoubtedly, each new season will see a number of other choices appear on the market—but will probably *not* see the prices go down. Still, there is some mighty good eating here in conveniently small packages that provide fine essential nourishment on the trail.

Although cost is certainly a major factor in determining which foods will make up the camp menu, the sheer bulk of the supply load must be considered when planning a very long trip. If resupply along the way is not practical, the party will have to carry everything it needs. In such an instance, the size and weight of the stores will matter more than relatively higher cost. A few years ago I had the opportunity to hike almost the whole length of Alaska's Wrangell Mountain Range. The trip was supported by a single air drop midway along our course, but without the most modern freeze-dried products it would have been impossible. The food costs were roughly the same as if we had eaten in high-class restaurants, but the whole experience was one of the greatest adventures I've ever undertaken—well worth the price!

Between the supermarket foods and the backpack goodies, any party should be able to plan a menu that will give plenty of energy and a good balance of the important nutrients, and still fall within their budget. If that is how the trip works out, you've done your planning well!

7

Recipes

Once the food list has been completed, the food purchased and packed, and a few miles of trail pushed behind, it remains for the camp cook to put the foods together in a pleasing and attractive fashion. Most trail meals lend themselves to simple preparation, but even the best of foods will turn into a meaningless glop if slopped together and cooked haphazardly. A little time and care will produce some really beautiful trail meals.

The special foods, of course, have been designed for ease in fixing, with little latitude for creativity. If the directions are followed with even minimal care, meals will turn out fine.

Many of the following recipes will require some

premeasuring and packaging at home. In such cases
the mixture is carried in a single plastic bag on
which the name of the dish has been written. (It's
amazing how alike meals can look before they have
been reconstituted and cooked!) If there are any
special cooking directions, or if the cook isn't familiar
with a particular combination, it is a good idea to
jot the instructions down on a slip of paper and tuck
it in the bag as well. Dishes that require more than
one step of preparation will have the ingredients
for each step in a separate bag, but the bags may
be packed together. For example, a backpack omelette will have the egg and milk in one bag, onions
and mushrooms in another, and cheese in a third—
all contained in a single outer bag. That way the
dish can be pulled from the food bag as one unit,
with only water required for preparation. It is a
good idea, incidentally, to have three nylon food
bags in the pack, one for each type of meal. Breakfasts go in one, lunches in another, and dinners in
the third. This way it isn't necessary to drag out
the whole food supply for a trail lunch.

In camp, the three food bags should be stowed
so that hungry little varmints can't get at them.
The most acceptable method is to hang the food
from a tree or suspend it on a line between two
trees. If there are bear around, it should be hung
ten or twelve feet up to discourage the larger
scroungers. It is poor practice to keep food in the
tent while the party sleeps. If a bear decides to eat

your dinner, he will come and get it, creating a confrontation in the confined spaces of your tent. The tent will become much less confining momentarily, as he rips it to ribbons to find the goodies. Bears are usually less a problem than raccoons, skunks, and other smaller fellows, but all can be a nuisance.

If a serious threat is posed by an animal with a strong desire for the food stores, discretion becomes the better part of valor. Let them have the food! Sometimes the animal can be frightened off by the mere presence of humans; a little added noise usually helps. But if the animal decides to fight for the food, retreat in haste. In many parts of the country the raccoons and skunks are rabid, and even a minor bite can have tragic consequences. Properly stored food, securely wrapped to limit the scent, is the best insurance against such trouble.

Several of the recipes included in this book require eggs or milk to prepare, in particular the cake and biscuit mixes you will bake in the backpack oven. It isn't feasible to carry real milk or fresh eggs, but the dehydrated products work fine. They require a little premixing before the recipe is attempted, so mix them in the following manner:

EGGS—for recipes
1 oz. dehydrated egg
1 oz. cold water
Mix thoroughly and allow to stand for 5 minutes. Equals 1 whole egg.

MILK—for recipes (not for drinking)
⅓ cup nonfat dry milk
1 cup cold water
¼ tsp. vegetable oil

Mix thoroughly and allow to stand for 1 minute.
Equals 1 cup milk.

Milk for drinking, pouring on cereal, etc., is made according to package directions, but the oil is omitted. Oil is added to the cooking milk to make a richer finished product and balance the original recipe.

With these little mixing details out of the way, let's get on with the recipes that will bring good flavors and easy eatin' to the trail camp.

BREAKFAST RECIPES

BASIC SCRAMBLED EGGS

Premix and package:
2 oz. dehydrated eggs
1 oz. nonfat dry milk
¼ oz. onion flakes

Mix with water to the consistency of thick batter, let stand 5 minutes. Pour into a greased frying pan and cook until the fluffy eggs are nearly dry. Stir almost constantly to get the mix to fluff. Salt and pepper to taste. Serves 2.

BACKPACK OMELETTE

Premix and package:
2 oz. dehydrated egg
1 oz. dry milk

Package separately:
¼ oz. onion flakes
¼ oz. dried mushrooms

Third package:
1 oz. cheese food

Let onion and mushrooms stand 15 minutes in 1 cup water. When softened, mix in egg and milk to form batter. Pour into greased frying pan and cook without stirring for about 3 minutes. Spread cheese over egg, fold edges of egg over the cheese to make a flat roll. Cover and cook about 3 more minutes until done. Season to taste. Serves 2.

BASIC OATMEAL

Premeasure and package:
1 cup dry oatmeal

Package separately:
½ cup dry milk

In 2 cups of boiling water bring oatmeal just to a boil, then reduce heat. Meanwhile mix milk with 1 cup cold water and let stand. When oatmeal is soft and thick, pour cold milk over and let simmer until milk is warm. The warmed milk thins the oatmeal and keeps it warm much longer. Serve with honey. Serves 2.

SUPER OATMEAL BREAKFAST

Premeasure and package:
1 cup dry oatmeal

Package separately:
½ cup dry milk
2 oz. raisins
¼ tsp. powdered cinnamon

Cook oatmeal according to package directions; when done, stir in 1 cup water, dry milk, raisins, and cinnamon. Simmer for about 5 minutes, stirring occasionally, until all is warm. Serve with honey or brown sugar. Serves 2.

BREAKFAST RICE

Premeasure and package:
1 cup rice
¼ tsp. salt

Package separately:
¼ oz. onion flakes
½ oz. ham-flavored vegetable protein

Boil rice in 1 cup water, remove from heat and let
stand according to package directions. Meanwhile,
reconstitute onion and vegetable protein in 1 cup of
water, warm if possible, for 15 minutes. Drain. Mix
rice and other ingredients, fry in greased skillet
only until rice is nicely browned. Serves 2.

SWEET MORNING RICE

Premeasure and package:
1 cup rice
1 oz. chopped dried apple

Package separately:
2 oz. raisins
½ tsp. cinnamon
1 oz. brown sugar

Boil rice in 1 cup *unsalted* water, remove from heat. Immediately stir in raisin, sugar, and cinnamon. Cover and let stand until rice is fluffy. This filling breakfast needs no other sweetener. Serves 2.

NUTTY OATMEAL

Premeasure and package:
1 cup oatmeal
½ cup nonfat dry milk
¼ tsp. salt

Package separately:
1 oz. chopped dates
1 oz. chopped nut meats (unsalted)
1 oz. brown sugar

Boil oatmeal-milk mix in 2½ cups water, remove from heat. Stir in dates, nuts, and sugar. Return to low heat and simmer about 3 minutes, stirring occasionally. Hearty and filling, this dish needs nothing further. Serves 2.

BREAKFAST HASH BROWNS

Premeasure and package:
3 oz. dehydrated hash browns
½ oz. onion flakes

For really tender, fresh-flavored potatoes, soak overnight in 1 cup cold water. (Cover to keep out sticks, bugs, leaves, etc.) Fry in a greased skillet until golden brown and crisp. Season to taste. Serves 2.

POTATO PATTIES

Premeasure and package:
⅔ cup instant mashed potatoes
⅓ cup dry milk
¼ tsp. salt
¼ tsp. onion salt

Package separately:
1 tbsp. margarine

Stir 2 cups cold water into potato mix. (It will be thicker than regular mashed potatoes.) Stir in margarine, form into 4-inch patties. Fry in a greased skillet until crispy brown, turn and repeat on second side. Serves 2.

BREAKFAST RINGS

Premeasure and package:
½ cup instant mashed potatoes
¼ cup dry milk
¼ tsp. salt

Package separately:
½ cup dehydrated eggs
¼ tsp. onion flakes

Third package:
1 tbsp. margarine

Mix potato and milk mix with 1 cup water; set aside. Mix egg and onion with enough water to make a thick batter. In a greased frying pan, form the potato mixture into two thick 4-inch doughnuts. Immediately pour the egg mix into the hole in the center of each. When potato is browned, turn each ring as a unit, cooking the second side until it is brown. Attractive and hearty. Serves 2.

BASIC HOTCAKES

Premeasure and package:
1 cup add-water-only pancake mix

Package separately:
2 oz. honey or syrup

Mix pancake flour with about ¾ cup of water. Stir only until bubbles appear and all dry mix is liquified. Don't overmix! Fry on hot skillet until large bubbles appear on the hotcake. Turn and cook until done. Serve with honey or syrup. Makes about 6 4-inch hotcakes.

SUPER HOTCAKES

Premeasure and package:
1 cup add-water-only pancake mix
¼ cup dry milk

Package separately:
2 oz. honey or syrup

Third package:
1 oz. vegetable oil

Forage for:
¼ cup fresh blackberries or huckleberries

Stir pancake mix and milk into about 1 cup water, add vegetable oil. In season, add fresh berries for tiny explosions of flavor. Cook as regular hotcakes, but don't overcook. Serve with honey or syrup if desired. Makes about 6 4-inch cakes.

GREEN AND GOLD

Premix and package:
½ cup dehydrated eggs
¼ tsp. salt

Forage for:
2 cups fresh nettle, dock, or other greens

Boil fresh greens about 5 minutes, set aside. Mix egg with ½ cup water, fry as for scrambled eggs in greased skillet. Drain greens, arrange in a flat layer on plate. Place eggs in a thick layer over greens, season to taste. A filling and refreshing way to start the day in camp. Serves 2.

BREAKFAST PASTRIES

Premeasure and package:
1 cup breakfast cake mix
¼ cup dried apple

Package separately:
1 oz. dehydrated egg
¼ cup dry milk

Third package:
1 tbsp. margarine

Mix egg and milk with about ½ cup water, set aside. Following package directions, and using above mix both for milk and egg, blend batter with margarine. Bake in ring-style backpack oven about 20 minutes, or according to directions, depending on cake type and brand. Often overlooked, this is a rather elegant breakfast that is relatively easy to prepare on the trail. Serves 2 or more.

BREAKFAST SALAD

Premeasure and package:
1 cup rice
¼ tsp. salt

Package separately:
1 oz. ham-flavored TVP®

Third package:
2 hard-boiled eggs

Cook rice according to directions. Meanwhile, put TVP® in 1 cup boiling water and set aside for 10 minutes. Peel and chop eggs. Drain TVP® and mix all ingredients together. Allow to cool, season to taste. (NOTE: if this is to be served the first morning out, carry 2 tbsps. of mayonnaise-type dressing along, as it adds a sparkling flavor to the breakfast salad.)

BREAKFAST GORP

(To be made at home and carried as is for breakfast snacking.)

Premix and bag:
½ cups raisins
½ cup chopped nuts
½ cup chopped dates

½ cup apple slices (dried)
1 tbsp. brown sugar
½ tsp. cinnamon

Mix all well in a plastic bag. This mix can be eaten out of hand or stirred into oatmeal, rice, or even hot-cake batter. Makes about 16 ounces.

THE SUPER-DUPER OMELETTE

Premeasure and package:
½ cup dehydrated egg
¼ tsp. salt
1 tsp. dry milk

Package separately:
½ tsp. onion flakes
½ oz. dried mushrooms

Third package:
¼ cup dry white wine

Separately:
1 packet sour cream mix

Put onion and mushroom in a cup of warm water; set aside. Mix the egg and milk mix with the wine and ¼ cup water. Mix the sour cream as per packet directions. Pour mixed eggs in greased skillet at moderate heat. Drain onions and mushrooms and sprinkle over center of egg. Spread sour cream on top, fold side of egg over to form a flat roll. Cover and cook at reduced heat about 8 minutes. Serves 2 in elegant style.

SPANISH EGG BREAKFAST

(Fresh ingredients limit this to an overnight trip.)

3 fresh eggs
½ cup chopped green pepper
½ cup chopped fresh onion
¼ cup dry milk
¼ cup chopped pepperoni

Mix dry milk with ¼ cup water, blend all ingredients together. Fry in a greased skillet, stirring constantly, until eggs are done. Season to taste. Serves 2. NOTE: Carry fresh eggs, broken, in small plastic jar or bottle.

POTATO ROUNDIES

(Weight and special equipment limit this to the weekend trip.)

1 large, fresh potato
½ cup chopped bacon

Wash the fresh potato and grate onto a paper towel. Heat ¼ cup of oil until almost smoking in skillet. Mix potatoes and bacon, form into thin patties, and fry until edges of potato curl. Drain, season and serve. Serves 2.

On first-day or campground breakfasts, take advantage of fresh fruits, eggs, fresh potatoes, or meats. By limiting the conventional trail foods to trail meals it is possible to add untold variety to the menu at breakfast time.

Lunch meals, for the most part, are hastily devised and quickly eaten along the trail. If the day's itinerary calls for short shuttles out of a base camp, any of the larger dinner meals can be substituted at noon. That often allows the party to take a lighter supper and perhaps a bedtime snack to make up the day's calorie requirements. On the trail, though, the ideal lunch will be reasonably light, easy to prepare, and extra digestible. If a hardy lunch is planned, the party will probably want to lounge around for a while instead of attacking the trail with a heavy stomach.

LUNCH RECIPES

THE SOUP SNACK

Premeasure and package:
1 oz. (1 pkt.) soup mix

Package separately:
4 pilot bread crackers
2 oz. tube cheese spread or peanut butter

Boil soup according to package directions. Serve with spread pilot bread and a hot drink. Most commercial soup packets make 4-6 cups of soup, too much for a pair of hikers. Divide the packet into 2 lunches with diet scale and plastic bag.

HEARTY LUNCH SOUP

Premeasure and package:
1 oz. vegetable soup mix
4 oz. enriched egg noodles
¼ tsp. salt.

Bring all ingredients to a boil in 3 cups of water, then allow to simmer for 10 minutes. The soup is particularly rich because of the carbohydrates included in the liquid. Serve with crackers and flavored drink. Serves 2.

BIFFY BURGERS

Premeasure and package:
2 oz. beef-flavored TVP®

Package separately:
8 pilot bread crackers

Third package:
2 oz. cheese spread

Bring 1 cup water to a boil, add TVP® and let simmer until fully reconstituted. Drain and add cheese spread to the hot TVP®. Continue to heat over low flame until cheese and TVP® are melted together. Spread between pilot bread crackers as miniature cheeseburger sandwiches. Serves 2. The pot is a little hard to clean after this, but the neat flavor and high nutritional value makes it worthwhile.

LUNCHEON GORP

Premeasure and package:
1 cup raisins
1 cup cocktail peanuts
½ cup coated chocolates (M&M®)
½ cup mixed nuts

This universal finger-food provides high energy with great ease. This recipe makes 24 oz. Each hiker should have a minimum of 6 oz. daily, more if gorp will be used for some lunches.

HI-CARBO GORP

(This is a better lunch choice, since the carbohydrate content is considerably higher than the above all-purpose mix.)

1 cup raisins
½ cup mixed nuts
1 cup dried fruits (apples, pears, etc.)
1 cup coated chocolate drops

Makes about 28 oz.

HEARTY LUNCHEON STEW

Premeasure and package:
2 oz. dehydrated stew vegetables
1 oz. (1 pkt.) onion soup mix
¼ tsp. salt

Package separately:
4 oz. tin vienna sausages

Forage for:
Wild mint (optional)

Bring stew vegetables and soup mix to a boil, then simmer about ten minutes. Add vienna sausages about 3 minutes before serving. Top with a couple of sprigs of fresh wild mint for a refreshing change. Serves 2.

FRIDAY LUNCHEON

Premeasure and package:
1 packet potato soup mix

½ cup dry milk
½ tsp. salt
1 oz. dehydrated corn

Package separately:
6½ oz.-tin small clams

Bring soup mix and other ingredients to a boil in 3 cups water; reduce heat and simmer 15 minutes. Add clams, simmer another 5 minutes. Serve with crackers. Serves 2.

RICE NOONER

Premeasure and package:
1 cup rice
1 oz. raisins
1 oz. dehydrated apple slices

Package separately:
2 oz. brown sugar

Separately:
1 tbsp. margarine

Bring rice and fruit to a boil in 1½ cups of water, cover and reduce heat. When rice is fluffy, mix in margarine and sugar. Serve with cold drink. Serves 2.

LUNCH DUNKERS

(Fresh ingredients limit this to weekend outings.)

1 pkt. onion soup mix
1 cube beef bouillon
2 small french rolls
2 oz. packaged beef lunch meat

Boil soup and bouillon in 1½ cups water. Slice french rolls and make beef sandwiches. Use soup both as a french dip and a hot lunchtime drink. Serves 2.

CHICK 'N' DUMPINS

Premeasure and package:
½ cup pancake mix
¼ cup dry milk
¼ tsp. salt

Package separately:
1 pkt. chicken-noodle soup mix

Bring soup to a boil, according to packet directions, lower heat, and simmer. Meanwhile, mix pancake and milk batter with ½ cup water to make very thick batter. Spoon the batter into the soup in large lumps and allow to simmer for about 10 minutes, or until dumplings are done. Serves 2 or more.

RICE MEDLEY

Premeasure and package:
1 cup rice
½ tsp. salt

Package separately:
2 oz. dehydrated mixed vegetables
1 pkt. beef gravy mix

Boil rice in 1 cup water, cover and set aside. In 1 cup water mix gravy and vegetables, heat and allow to simmer until vegetables are soft. Pour vegetables in gravy over rice, stir well, and serve. Heavy lunch for 2.

CATTAIL DANDY LUNCH

Premeasure and package:
½ package leek soup mix
¼ cup dry milk

Forage for:
1 cup fresh cattail shoots, cut into
½-inch sections

Boil soup and milk mix in 2 cups water, reduce heat and simmer 10 minutes. About 3 minutes before serving, add cattail shoots. Hearty soup serves 2.

TRAIL TORTILLAS

Premeasure and package:
¾ cup pancake mix
¼ cup dry milk

Package separately:
1 oz. beef-flavored vegetable protein
½ oz. onion flakes
¼ tsp. chili powder

Mix pancake and milk with 1 cup water. Bake 2 large, thin hotcakes in a greased skillet. Meanwhile, add vegetable protein and other ingredients to ½ cup of hot water and set aside. Roll half the vegetable protein mix in each of the hotcakes, pour the remaining juice over and serve. Serves 2.

LUNCH HOTSIES

Premeasure and package:
1 cup rice
¼ tsp. salt

Package separately:
1 pkt. Chili seasoning mix
1 oz. beef-flavored TVP®

Boil rice in 1 cup water, cover, and remove from heat. In 1 cup water, mix chili seasoning and TVP® —do not boil, but heat; let stand 10 minutes. Pour chili-TVP® mix over rice and stir in. Great flavor in a hurry. Serves 2 or more.

DUCKABUSH DELIGHT

Premeasure and package:
4 oz. enriched egg noodles
2 oz. beef-textured vegetable protein
½ pkt. meat loaf seasoning mix
½ tsp. salt

Bring 3 cups of water to a boil, add all ingredients, and reduce heat. Stir often while simmering, about 15 minutes. Serve with pilot bread crackers. Serves 2 large appetites.

TRAIL SPAGHETTI

Premeasure and package:
4 oz. spaghetti
2 oz. beef-flavored TVP®
2 oz. dehydrated tomato flakes

Bring 2 cups water to a boil, add all ingredients and reduce heat. Let simmer for about 10 minutes. Serves 2.

CREAMY CHICKEN GUMBO

Premeasure and package:
1 pkt. tomato-vegetable soup mix
¼ cup dry milk
2 oz. elbow macaroni

Package separately:
6½-oz. tin of boned chicken

Cook soup mix, milk, and macaroni in 3 cups water. Simmer about 5 minutes, add boned chicken and simmer another 5 minutes. Serves 2-3.

FRUITY LUNCH CAKES

Premeasure and package:
½ cup hotcake mix
¼ cup dry milk
1 tbsp. sugar

Package separately:
½ cup mixed dried fruit
2 tbsp. brown sugar

Mix pancake packet with ¾ cup water. Cook hot-cakes normally, set aside. Put ¼ cup water in a small saucepan and cook fruit and sugar mixture until thick and syrupy; pour over the cooled hot-cakes. Very high in carbohydrates for quick trail energy. Messy, but great. Makes 4 lunch cakes.

LUNCH RICE SALAD

Premeasure and package:
1 cup rice
¼ tsp. salt

Package separately:
¼ cup chopped nuts
¼ cup chopped dates and raisins

At breakfast time, cook rice and set aside to cool. Mix chopped fruit and nuts in thoroughly, and package in a plastic bag. At lunchtime, only the prepared salad and a spoon are necessary to unpack. Serves 2.

QUICK GREEN LUNCH

Premeasure and package:
1 oz. ham-flavored TVP®
1 oz. dehydrated egg

Forage for:
    3 cups washed and chopped edible greens:
    dandelion, dock, nettle, etc.

Drop greens in boiling water and cook for about
5 minutes. Drain about half the water, stir in the
TVP® and egg mix. Simmer for about 8 minutes,
then drain, careful not to lose the TVP® or the egg,
which will cook into small nuggets. Serve with
crackers, steaming hot. Serves 2.

These are just a few of the lunch possibilities;
they depend on generally available supermarket
foods. If you wish to use special freeze-dried lunches,
fresh meat or cheese for sandwiches, or more ambi-
tious dishes, you can expand your noon options
many times. If time is not a factor, almost any of
the suppertime meals can be reduced in size and
served for the noon meal on the trail. The luncheon
latitude is limited only by the energy and ambition
of the chef.

The dinner meal is normally the largest and most
complicated of the day. The dishes in this section
are primarily designed to be *part* of your supper,
not the whole thing. If appetites are not ravenous,
a single bowl of chili over rice or a Helper® dinner
might be enough. More often, however, dinner will
consist of three or four separate dishes cooked over
a period of two hours or so. In this way dinner does
not become an unbearable burden for the chef, and
can be an extended social hour for the party. After

the camp is established and the essential chores completed, the long dinner hour can serve to keep everyone from being bored. More important, it is during this special time that the finest memories are built and lifetime friendships affirmed.

DINNER RECIPES

CHILI DIABLO AND RICE

Premeasure and package:
1 cup rice
¼ tsp. salt

Package separately:
1 pkt. chili seasoning
2 oz. beef-textured vegetable protein
2 oz. dehydrated tomato flakes

Third package:
1 10-ounce tin of real beef

Bring rice to a boil in 1 cup of water, cover and set aside. In a saucepan, cook the chili seasonings, vegetable protein, and seasoning in 1½ cups water until thickened. Stir the tinned beef into the thickened sauce and simmer for about 5 minutes. Put the rice on the plate, making a well in the center, and pour the beef and sauce over it. Simple but superb in the evening camp. Serves 2.

SPUDS 'N' GRAVY

Premeasure and package:
1 cup instant mashed potatoes
½ cup dry milk
½ tsp. salt

Package separately:
1 pkt. gravy mix

To the potato and milk mix add ½ cup boiling water. Stir well, adjusting the water as required to achieve the desired consistency. Meanwhile, stir the gravy mix into 1 cup of water according to packet directions. Serves 2 as a side to meat or other dishes.

CHINESE FRIED RICE

Premeasure and package:
1 cup rice
¼ tsp. salt

Package separately:
1 oz. dehydrated vegetables
½ tsp. onion flakes

Third package:
3½ oz. tin of tiny shrimp

Bring rice to a boil, cover and set aside. In 1 cup of warm water rehydrate the onions and vegetables. When they are soft, mix drained vegetables and rice in a greased skillet until it begins to brown. Add the shrimp and continue to fry until done. 1½ ounce of soy sauce (available in individual plastic packets) will greatly enhance the flavor. Serves 2 as a main or side dish.

CHIWAUKUM CHOW MEIN

(May be cooked in skillet, but wok produces better dish.)

Premeasure and package:
4 oz. enriched Chinese-style noodles
2 oz. stew vegetables

Package separately:
2 oz. beef jerky
1 tsp. onion flakes

Cook noodles and vegetables in 4 cups boiling water. Drain and set aside. Soften jerky and onions in just enough warm water to cover. When soft, drain and combine with noodles and vegetables. Heat a little vegetable oil in a frying pan until nearly smoking; very quickly stir-fry the noodle-meat mixture until it is beginning to brown and crisp. Serve immediately. Serves 2-3.

BANNOCK BREAD

Premeasure and package:
4 cups flour
6 tbsp. sugar
1 tsp. salt
4 tsps. baking powder
¼ cup dry milk

Package separately:
⅓ cup shortening

Mix all dry ingredients, cream in shortening with a fork. Add water until dough has no dry spots but is not soggy. Press into a round cake about 1-inch thick, and lay in a hot, greased skillet. Cook until bottom is brown, then turn and cook second side in the same manner. If an open fire is used, this traditional bread is often finished by tipping the pan toward the fire, letting the direct heat warm and brown the top. The ingredients are a bit heavy, but the bannock is super for a weekender or other short outing. Serves 4.

BROWN WHEEL BREAD

(A relic of the old "grub" camping days, this smoky-flavored treat is well worth the added weight. Because of the fresh bacon, it is a weekender.)

Premeasure and package:
2 cups flour
2 tbsps. sugar
2 tsps. salt
4 tsps. baking powder
¾ cup dry milk

Package separately:
6 slices bacon

Cut bacon slices in half and cook until about half done. Arrange in the skillet like spokes of a wheel. Mix the dry ingredients with 1 cup of water to make a thin batter. Pour over the bacon and cook for about 12 minutes or until bottom begins to brown. Turn the loaf over and cook another 12 minutes or until a straw thrust into the bread comes out dry. Serves 4.

HELPER® DINNERS

(This recipe works for the dozen or so Helper® packaged meals at the store. It is cooked in a single pot and makes a surprisingly good dinner for about 8 oz. of backpack weight.)

Premeasure and package:
½ package Helper® dinner
2 oz. beef TVP®

Pour all ingredients into necessary amount of water. (See package directions; totals vary according to meal type.) To this add ½ cup of water, which will be absorbed by the TVP®. Cook until all potatoes and vegetables are tender and the TVP® fully reconstituted. Too little water will make it very salty. Serves 2.

RICH HUNTER'S STEW

Premeasure and package:
1 cup dehydrated diced potatoes
4 oz. dehydrated stew vegetables
½ tsp. salt
1 pkt. onion soup mix

Package separately:
1 10-oz. tin real beef

Bring all dry ingredients to boiling in 4 cups of water. Reduce heat and simmer until all are tender. Add chunks of beef and simmer another 10 minutes. Serves 4.

GENTLY JOHNNIE STEW

Premeasure and package:
6 oz. dehydrated hash browns
2 oz. dehydrated stew vegetables

2 oz. tomato flakes
2 oz. beef-flavored TVP®

Cook all ingredients in 4 cups water. Need not boil, but this stew must simmer at least 20 minutes to enrich the flavor. Serves 4.

OLD FASHIONED HASH

Premeasure and package:
6 oz. dehydrated hash browns
2 oz. tomato flakes
2 oz. onion flakes

Packaged separately:
6½-oz. tin corned beef

Cook dry ingredients in 2½ cups of water until all are soft. As the mixture simmers, stir in corned beef, carefully mashing all ingredients together with a fork. Serves 4, or ½ can be reserved for breakfast in a 2-person camp.

TAMALE PIE

Premeasure and package:
1 cup pancake mix
½ cup dry milk
½ tsp. salt

Package separately:
4 oz. beef-textured vegetable protein
2 oz. tomato flakes
1 tsp. onion flakes

Third package:
2 oz. cheese food

Mix dry ingredients with 1¼ cups water to make batter; cook into standard pancakes. Soak vegetable protein, tomato, and onion in 1 cup water until soft, then heat to boiling. Spoon meaty tomato mix over hotcakes, crumble cheese on top, and roll them up. Pour the remaining tomato sauce over. Serves 2-3.

CAMP MUFFINS

Premeasure and package:
1 cup instant pancake mix
¼ cup sugar
1 oz. dehydrated egg

Package separately:
1 tbsp. vegetable oil

Mix dry ingredients with just ¼ cup water, stir in oil. Spoon into lightly greased skillet, cover tightly with foil, and cook over low heat until muffins are done. The shapes will be erratic, but the flavor great. Makes 6 muffins.

TOASTITE SANDWICHES

(For the campground or treats at the trail-head—gear too heavy for backpacking.)

For each sandwich:
2 slices whole wheat bread
1 oz. peanut butter
1 oz. jam

Put jam and peanut butter in the middle of a slice of bread (not spread as a normal sandwich), put the second slice on top, and clamp it all firmly in the toastite. Cook over an open fire until the bread is nicely browned. Plan to make plenty of them—they go fast!

MEATY TOASTITE SANDWICHES

For each sandwich:
2 slices bread
2 oz. cubed beef or other meat
1 oz. gravy

As before, put the meat and gravy mix in the middle of the bread, cover with the second slice, and clamp in the toastite. Cook over an open fire until done. These are rich and filling. For variety, add chopped onion, green pepper, or a spoon of precooked vegetable to the meat mix.

DINNER PANCAKES

Premeasure and package:
1 cup pancake mix
¼ cup dry milk

Package separately:
2 oz. dehydrated egg
1 oz. dry milk

Third package:
1 pkt. gravy mix

Mix pancake mix with 1 cup water, cook dollar-size pancakes, and set aside. Combine gravy mix with 1 cup water and heat according to package directions. Mix egg and milk mix with ½ cup water to make very thin batter. Dip pancakes in batter, fry in hot skillet until browned. Cooked much like french toast, the dollar cakes are excellent when gravy is poured over them, having high calorie, carbohydrate, and protein content. Makes about a dozen dollar cakes.

SPECIAL BEEF SOUP

Premeasure and package:
1 pkt. vegetable beef soup
2 oz. dehydrated stew vegetables

1 oz. dehydrated corn
1 cube beef bouillon
2 oz. freeze-dried beef

Package separately:
2 oz. grated parmesan cheese

Bring 5 cups water to a boil. Add all ingredients except cheese, reduce heat, and simmer for 15 minutes. Sprinkle cheese over each bowl. This hearty dinner soup will feed 3-4.

TRAIL GOULASH

Premeasure and package:
4 oz. elbow macaroni
2 oz. stew vegetables
2 oz. tomato flakes
1 pkt. tomato beef soup

Package separately:
4 oz. beef TVP®

Put TVP® in 1 cup warm water and set aside. Add all dry ingredients to 3 cups of boiling water; simmer for 15 minutes. Add the drained TVP® and simmer for an additional 5 minutes. Serves 2.

TUNA AND NOODLES

Premeasure and package:
4 oz. enriched egg noodles
2 oz. dehydrated peas
1 pkt. chicken-noodle soup mix

Package separately:
6½-oz. tin flaked tuna

Add all dry ingredients to 2½ cups boiling water. Simmer until noodles are soft, about 10 min. Add the tuna and simmer an additional 5 minutes. Best served over toast or biscuits if possible. Serves 2-3, more if toast or biscuits are available.

CREAMED CHICKEN ON RICE

Premeasure and package:
1 cup rice
½ tsp. salt

Package separately:
1 oz. leek soup mix
1 tsp. onion flakes

Third package:
6½-oz. tin boned chicken

Cook rice in 1 cup of water, cover and set aside. Mix soup mix and onion with 1 cup water, simmer until thickened. Add chicken to this sauce, simmering an additional 5 minutes. Serve chicken and sauce over the rice. Serves 2 or more.

COWPUNCHER'S CAKE

(Make bannock bread as per previous recipe.)

Premeasure and package:
4 oz. beef TVP®
1 pkt. Chili seasoning
2 oz. tomato flakes

Package separately:
2 oz. cheese food

Separately:
1 oz. onion flakes

Cook TVP®, seasoning, and tomato flakes in 1½ cups water. Meanwhile add onion flakes to ½ cup warm water. Pour TVP® and sauce over broken chunks of bannock bread, crumble cheese on top, and sprinkle drained, rehydrated onion over all. Serves 2 or more.

FLAVORED NOODLE DISHES

Premeasure and package:
½ pkt. Top-Ramen® noodles

Prepare, with boiling water, according to package directions. Half the standard package will make a fine side dish for two. Some varieties have a separate flavor packet to be added after the noodles are cooked. In this case divide the flavor mix as well.

A great many of the modern "convenience" foods in the supermarket can be used for main courses or side dishes on the trail. The popular macaroni-and-cheese dinners, for example, are fine as a side, but usually must be divided and packaged according to the size of the party. The diet scale and a couple of small plastic bags will accomplish that easily.

A whole new genre of eating treats has recently appeared for the steady backpacker, mostly because of the development of the lightweight oven. By using the various cake mixes and appropriate utensils, desserts never before available are now child's play along the trail. They will require the use of whole egg powders and nonfat dry milk in many instances, but they are quite possible.

It would be pointless to repeat the directions here, since practically every individual mix is different. The same is true of the many drink mixes crowding the grocer's shelves; there are just too many and they are all too simple to require any explanation here.

The imaginative backpacker can choose a completely different meal for every day he spends on the trail, even if the stay will be for many weeks. The freeze-dried specialties alone embrace perhaps a hundred different meals and the supermarket foods will provide several hundred more. About the only kind of food that is unsuited for the trail is that which is either too heavy or that which needs refrigeration. That leaves literally hundreds of potential choices for the group planning an outing.

Probably the only kind of food that we have yet to discuss—and that lends itself to trail cookery— is the "freebie" that grows along the pathway.

12

The Wild Ones

The purpose of a wilderness experience is to put the pressures and commonplaces of society behind in favor of an exciting adventure. To appreciate fully the value of the exercise, it is necessary to establish a personal relationship with the environmental elements, to become an honest part of the land that surrounds us. The feel of cold, rushing brook water and the smells of sun-baked soil are just as important to the overall experience as the faroff view of a rugged mountain or the majesty of a towering forest. There is probably no more intimate way to become involved in the wilderness than to use some of it for the sustenance of life.

The art of foraging—collecting and eating wild

plants—has undergone a renaissance in the past few years. No longer the necessity it was in the past, foraging is helping thousands of people to discovering the enjoyments of self-sufficiency. Hundreds of books have been written on the subject, and all around the country special foraging classes have sprung up at community colleges, park departments, and outdoor clubs. The use of wild plants can enrich the outing for everyone concerned, but there are drawbacks as well as advantages.

Among the advantages is the enjoyment of good food that need not be carried on the back. Many of the better wild edibles can be found practically anywhere, can be cooked very easily over a backpack stove, and provide a wealth of natural vitamins and minerals that cannot be found in regular trail foods. Dandelion, for example, has probably more vitamin A than any other plant on earth. In the days when trail and camp dinners were a way of life, a few green plants were added to the menu to prevent scurvy and other vitamin deficiency diseases. Darned few modern hikers are ever afflicted with rickets or scurvy, but the addition of a plate of steaming greens to the menu can help maintain a good vitamin balance. They also provide a freshness of flavor that is often absent from the backpack diet, and they are just a lot of fun to include.

The primary disadvantage of wild foods, of course, is the possibility of incorrect identification, leading to the ingestion of a potentially harmful plant. Of the 20,000-odd classified plants in North America, only about 2,000 are known to be edible. About the same number are deemed poisonous to some degree. That leaves around 15,000 plants about which we know nothing in terms of edibility. Obviously, proper identification of the beneficial plants is of the utmost importance to the forager.

A large number of otherwise responsible survival manuals describe an edibility test by which the safety of unknown plants may be determined. The test begins with putting a small amount of the subject plant in the mouth and immediately spitting it out. If there are no ill effects, another small sample is chewed and then spit out. If all goes well, a tiny piece is chewed and swallowed. Successively larger pieces are eaten at 12-hour intervals until the plant is deemed edible. The only piece of advice I can offer about this edibility test is DON'T TRY IT! You just might end up dead.

In the first place, if the plant in question were one of the hemlocks or water parsnips, the initial oral contact could leave enough of the poison mixed with saliva to cause death. If the plant contained any of the crystalline oxalic acids, the chewing stage would cause the barbed crystals to penetrate the lip and tongue tissue and massive swelling would result. Often the swelling is great enough to close the air passages and cause suffocation. Either way, not the plant but *we* have failed the test!

Even if the plant is edible, the test requires as

many as 96 hours to complete, and no other food could be taken during that period—hardly a practical approach to survival. Let the testing be done in the botanical laboratory and our selection of plants be guided by a combination of scientific data and human history. Within those parameters there are hundreds of useful and delicious plants to add to the trail menu.

On the subject of wild meats the choices are a lot easier. Although there may be a few poisonous fish or shellfish in a given locale, most wild meats are edible. Because many hikers and backpackers are not practicing hunters, we'll skip any reference to big game animals in this chapter. It is important to note that many large animals require a two or three day cooling period before they should be eaten, so that pretty well eliminates them from the hiking menu anyway. The majority of hikers will settle for an occasional trout, perch, or crawdaddy. (The exotic edible meats such as grubs, earthworms, rattlesnakes, and rodents will be totally ignored in this book. I have enough trouble with a ruffed grouse or a catfish!)

Actually, wild meats don't play much of a part in the hiking diet for quite another reason. Most of us are too busy soaking up the scenery, hiking from one place to another, and relaxing around an evening campfire to sacrifice the many hours required for securing wild game. We will concentrate on the edible plants that can augment the diet since they are relatively easy to collect, simple to prepare and cook, and seldom, if ever, bite back. Most of us don't have any strong food prejudices against the use of wild weeds, a statement that cannot be made in behalf of field mice and larvae!

Before we get to the dozen or so specific green plants that will be included here, it would be a good idea to look at the nuts and berries that can be found in many parts of the country. There are a few generalizations that are often made about berries (black or blue are all right, red sometimes OK, and white usually poisonous), but there is too much latitude in generalizations to be safe. If a specific berry is not known *by you* to be safe, don't eat it. The same is true of the many nuts around in the fall; some are good and some are definitely harmful. Know which is which before you put them in your stomach. If foraging is to be part of the hike activity, a reliable regional guidebook should be included in your specialized equipment. Coastal hikers should carry a key to the fishes and shellfish if those are to be included in the diet.

The wild foods should always be considered supplementary to the food list on the hike. Under no circumstances can we rely on collecting sufficient food to maintain our party; all the essential food must be carried on every trip. A lot of skinny nimrods have returned from some alpine lake absolutely famished because they relied on their fishing skill to fill the frying pan. By the same token, in an emergency a working knowledge of ten or twelve wild plants will fill the stomach much more reliably than expertise with a fly rod.

The following list of plants was chosen on the basis of universal distribution, easy identification, and good taste. In many cases very little is known about the nutritional value of the wild edible, but where a detailed analysis has been made the information appears with the plant description. Very few of the wild edibles are particularly high in calories, carbohydrates, or protein, and none has any significant fat content. The vitamin and mineral values may be widely varied by season and growing conditions, but most are fairly good. Fun and flavor are the primary reasons for adding them to the backpack inventory.

ARROWHEAD *(Sagittaria latifolia)*

A beautiful aquatic plant, the arrowhead is slender and graceful as it lifts from the clear water of the pond or lake. Regionally known as duck potato, tule potato, and wapato. The subsurface tubers are the edible portion, gathered in late summer and fall from the mud at the bottom of the pond. The flavor of the egg-sized tuber is superior to the finest Irish potatoes. The Lewis and Clark party survived the disastrous winter of 1805-6 by trading with bands of Columbia River Indians for stores of arrowhead.

Arrowhead is an aquatic perennial with a slim fleshy stem growing from a network of tubers in the

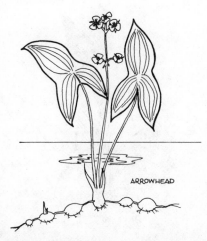

ARROWHEAD

soft underwater mud. Leaves have a striking arrow-head shape, are parallel-veined, and may be emergent or floating on the water. The tubers may be dislodged with the feet or a stick and will float to the surface. Peel the tubers and cook them as you would potatoes. They are delicious. No nutritional data are available, but they probably have high caloric and carbohydrate content.

BEAR GRASS *(Xerophyllum tenax)*

Bear grass is usually peculiar to mountainous alpine regions, but may occasionally be found at middle and low elevations. It is easily recognized by the thick upright stem and the showy spike of

BEARGRASS

white flowers. Even after the flowers are gone the large stalk is a good identifier. It was gathered by many Indian tribes both as food and a hardy weaving material. It got its name from the fact that bears relish the sweet, crunchy rootstocks.

Bear grass produces an erect flowering stalk from a mass of grasslike basal leaves. Small needle-shaped pointed leaves extend up the stalk to the conical flower head. They bloom only at long intervals, perhaps three or four years, so it is good to learn to recognize them from the basal clumps of grassy leaves. The fleshy root is pulled or dug from the ground, and is usually peeled before eating. The thick rootstock may be eaten raw or added to a stewpot. Either way it is delicious. No nutritional data are available.

CATTAIL *(Typhus latifolia)*

One of the most abundant aquatic weeds in North America, the cattail is also one of the most valuable as a wild food. It was used by early Indians as a food, confection, and construction material. The thick leaves were woven into baskets, sleeping mats, and even roof thatches. The roots were dug as staple foods, the leaf shoots used in season, and the pollen and thick spikes eaten in the fall.

The cattail can be recognized by its swampy habitat, the huge grass-like leaves, and the character-

CATTAIL

istic brown autumn spikes. In the spring and summer the leaves (usually paired) are pulled upright from the root. Below the point where the leaves separate is a rounded white shoot. Quite tender, the shoot resembles cucumber somewhat in flavor. It may be eaten raw or cooked. The root, often a large extensive system, has a tough brown skin and a fibrous layer beneath. The core, soft and pure white, is composed mainly of starches and can be cooked in any manner a potato can. It can be sautéed, fried, baked, boiled, mashed, and have gravy poured over it. The root is probably quite high both in calories and carbohydrates, but no analysis has been done. The pollen may be gathered in the fall and the yellow powder used in place of flour. It makes great hotcakes and biscuits. Most pollens are high in protein and B vitamins, and there is no reason to believe the cattail an exception.

CHICKWEED *(Stellaria media)*

A very common little weed, chickweed can be found in practically any soil or climate condition from northern Canada to the Mexican deserts. A familiar sight in any patch of woods, it can be used either as a salad ingredient or a cooked green.

The stems of chickweed are weak, often reclining, with many branches arising from the base. Stems are covered with fine hairs. The lower leaves have stems which are absent from the upper leaves. The tiny white flowers are borne in clusters at the top

CHICKWEED

of each stem. The plant is an annual but may persist all winter in warmer climates. It is especially good as a cooked green. No nutritional data are available for chickweed.

DANDELION *(Taraxacum officinale)*

The dandelion has been used in many cultures as a food for centuries; it is even cultivated in many places, but is properly called a wild edible plant. Anyone who cannot immediately recognize a dandelion must have spent his childhood on the moon.

The lion's-tooth leaves, thick root, and bright yellow flower on a hollow stem all serve to identify this common pest.

The young leaves may be eaten in a salad, but tend to become quite bitter with age. The older

DANDELION

leaves must be boiled, often in a couple of changes of water, to remove the bitterness. They are excellent as cooked greens and fine for eating raw. Dandelion leaves are an excellent source of vitamin A and a fair source of C vitamins. A 4-ounce serving has 42 calories and about 10.7 grams of carbohydrates, but fat and protein content are negligible. The root can be peeled and chopped, roasted until hard and brown, and then brewed into some of the finest caffein-free coffee substitute you have ever tasted. The root can also be used in soups and stews, but may tend to be quite bitter if it is old.

DOCK (*Rumex crispus* and related species)

Another terribly common weed, the various forms of dock have a whole bunch of aliases, including sheep sorrel, Indian tobacco, and curly dock. They are not, incidentally, suitable for smoking!

The various *Rumex* species have large green leaves that are smooth-edged, wavy, crisped, or any combination of these. The larger leaves form sheaths around the succulent stems, which are often tinged with red. The leaves have a definitely lumpy look and thrust up tall, ribbed stems that will bear many seedy fruits, which look like coarse tobacco when stripped from the stem.

DOCK

The leaves should be cut into strips and boiled
for about 5 minutes. They turn a very pale green
when cooked and taste something like asparagus.
Dock leaves are also very high in Vitamin A and
are an excellent source of Vitamin C, providing as
much as 119 mg. in a 100-gram sample. They are
lower than dandelion in calories and carbohydrates.

LAMB'S QUARTERS *(Chenopodium album)*

One of the most widely used of all wild edibles,
lamb's quarters is the *only* wild plant eaten by many
families. It grows almost anywhere soil has been
disturbed, particularly in backyard gardens and the
margins of plowed fields and orchards. It was not
widely used by the early Indians, but was a favorite
of the pioneers and settlers in this country. In some
locales it is known as pigweed, but should not be
confused with the more commonly known pigweed,
Amaranthus retroflexus.

Lamb's quarters prefers drier climates, but will
be found in varying abundance throughout the country. The leaves are roughly triangular with stepped
serrations, earning it another common euphemism,
goosefoot. The leaves are dark green above and
gray-green below, with a definitely gritty feel. In
mid-summer the central stalk will have large clusters
of tiny seeds, often as many as 50,000 seeds per
plant.

Lamb's quarters is best as a cooked green, although many people like it raw in a salad. After

LAMBSQUARTER

about 3 minutes of boiling the plant is surprisingly tender and among the most flavorful of greens. A 100-gram sample provides about 43 calories and 9.8 grams of carbohydrates, but is also low in protein and fat. It is an excellent source of vitamins A and C, but C is sharply reduced by cooking. The seeds can be collected and used, after some drying and grinding, as a rough flour or cereal grain. They are probably fair sources of B vitamins and plant protein, but no definitive analysis is available.

MILKWEED *(Asclepias)*
The several milkweeds common to this continent are all edible, but contain small quantities of toxins.

All are safe if eaten in reasonable quantities, having about the same toxins and levels as garden peas. Milkweed has a long and curious history both as a food and medicinal plant.

Milkweed is a common, fleshy-leaved plant that grows from 12 to 30 inches high and may be covered with soft hairs. The flowers are pink to red-purple and grow on large umbels on the upper part of the main stem. The flowers have conspicuous curved, horn-shaped appendages attached just above the reflexed petals. A warty pod develops on a stout, curved stem. The entire plant is filled with a milky latex fluid that flows profusely when the plant is cut or broken.

The young shoots and seed pods are the best part to eat. They may require boiling in two changes of water to remove the milky sap and any bitterness. No nutritional data are available for milkweed.

MINT *(Mentha canadensis and others)*

The common field and brook mints, some of which are escapees from cultivation, annually appear in large numbers in suitable, moist places. They are more a flavoring than an edible, but a few sprigs in a stew or salad will really enhance the flavor.

The mints are characteristically square-stemmed with opposite leaves rotating 90 degrees at regular

MINT

intervals. Most are quite small (to 12 inches) and
bear tiny purple flowers. They can be quickly iden-
tified by their pleasant odor.

Mint leaves may be dried in the sun for a day or
two and brewed into a refreshing tea. No nutritional
data are available.

STINGING NETTLE *(Urtica dioica)*

Distributed in the wetter locations throughout
the country, stinging nettles are among the easiest
of all plants to identify. If there is any doubt, a
quick brush of a finger across a leaf will prove the
plant is what it appears to be. The red welt and
painful sting are evidence enough.

It would seem odd that a plant that requires gloves
to pick could be edible, but stinging nettle is a delicious cooked green. A few seconds of boiling completely neutralize the oils that cause the sting.

The pale green leaves of the square-stalked nettle
are covered with tiny hairs that transfer the volatile
oils. The stem is likewise covered with hairs and can
deliver the sting. Rising to about 4 feet, the larger
plants are too tough to be much good, but young
plants are excellent. After boiling for just a couple
of minutes they turn a deep emerald green and taste
very much like spinach. No nutritional data are
available.

These are just a handful of the many fine plants

NETTLE

that can add to wilderness outings, offering new taste adventures and natural nutrients to the trail fare. A certain sense of self-sufficiency comes with learning to use the wild edibles, adding to the overall experience efficiency, economy, and plain fun.

If foraging appeals to you, and you want to add it to the list of activities to be enjoyed outdoors, get one of the excellent books on the subject at the library or outfitter. A few books that are national in scope can be purchased, among these a few that are completely illustrated—an essential to the novice forager. I would highly recommend *Field Guide to Edible Wild Plants,* by Brad Angier (Stackpole

Books), and westerners might enjoy my own book, *Why Wild Edibles,* from Pacific Search Books in Seattle. I am quite proud of the quality of the photos and illustrations in WWE, and I must note that the excellent all-color illustrations in Brad Angier's work are among the best tools the student of wild edibles can secure. Whatever the choice, take a reliable guidebook every time you go foraging, until you know each and every plant you will collect. The potential for tragedy is much too high to risk stumbling around in such a diversified field without a good source of accurate information.

The few representatives of the world of wild foods I have discussed are available in good quantities most of the year, yet our previous advice holds true: use them as a supplement to the formal food list you assemble for the outing. Don't rely on the harvest of wild foods as an exclusive (or even major) part of the trail diet. There are so many variables— seasons, soils, and growing conditions—that you just might come home hungry. Use the wild ones for an added treat, a spark of new flavor along the way, and they will reward your efforts well.

Index